**Herbert Puchta & Jeff Stranks**

G. Gerngross  C. Holzmann  P. Lewis-Jones

# American MORE! 1A

## COMBO   Student's Book

**NOTE FOR TEACHERS**

The pages of this Combo edition are numbered in the usual way in sequence throughout. Where the numbers are different from the original full edition Student's Book and Workbook pages, a second number is shown that looks like this: 23 . This is so that the page references in full edition teacher components such as the Teacher's Resource Book can be followed easily.

**editora ática**

Diretora-Geral Editoras Ática e Scipione
Vera Balhestero

Gerente Editorial e de Conteúdos Didáticos
Teresa Porto

Coordenador Editorial de Línguas Estrangeiras
Luiz Tonolli

Gerente de Qualidade e Suporte
Beatriz Mendes

**Assistente Editorial:** Danuza Dias Gonçalves
**Gerente de Revisão:** Hélia de Jesus Gonsaga
**Equipe de Revisão:** Célia da Silva Carvalho e Gloria Cunha
**Edição de Arte:** Erik Taketa e Mauro Fernandes
**Editoração Eletrônica:** A+ Comunicação

**American MORE! Combo 1A with CD-ROM/Audio CD**
Hebert Puchta & Jeff Stranks
G. Gerngross, C. Holzmann, P. Lewis-Jones

MORE! was originally published by Helbling Languages ©
Helbling Languages 2006
© Cambridge University Press and Helbling Languages 2010

This edition © Cambridge University Press, Helbling Languages
and Editora Ática S.A. 2011

Todos os direitos reservados.
Proibida a reprodução total ou parcial sem autorização
prévia e por escrito.

Direitos desta edição cedidos à Editora Ática S.A.
Av. Otaviano Alves de Lima, 4400
Freguesia do Ó – CEP 02909-900 – São Paulo – SP
Tel.: 4003-3061
www.atica.com.br / editora@atica.com.br

Dados Internacionais de Catalogação na Publicação (CIP)
(Câmara Brasileira do Livro, SP, Brasil)

> American more! : Combo : student's book / Herbert Puchta...[et al.]. -- 1. ed. -- São Paulo : Ática, 2011.
> Outros autores: Jeff Stranks, Gunther Gerngross, Christian Holzmann, Peter Lewis-Jones
> Obra em 8 v.
> Bibliografia.
>
> 1. Inglês (Ensino fundamental) I. Puchta, Herbert. II. Stranks, Jeff. III. Gerngross, Gunther. IV. Holzmann, Christian. V. Lewis-Jones, Peter.
>
> 11-13335    CDD-372.652

Índice para catálogo sistemático:
1. Inglês : Ensino Fundamental   372.652

2012
ISBN 978 85 08 15446 3 – American MORE! Combo 1A with CD-ROM and Audio CD
ISBN 978 85 08 14802 8 – American MORE! 1 Teacher's Book

Cód. da obra CL 738258

1ª edição
2ª impressão

Impressão e acabamento: Corprint Gráfica e Editora Ltda.

---

The authors would like to thank those people who have made significant contributions towards the final form of American MORE!

Oonagh Wade and Rosamund Cantalamessa for their expertise in working on the manuscripts, their useful suggestions for improvement, and the support we got from them.

Lucia Astuti and Markus Spielmann, Helbling Languages, Ron Ragsdale and James Dingle, Cambridge University Press, for their dedication to the project and innovative publishing vision.

Our designers, Amanda Hockin, Greg Sweetnam, Quantico, Craig Cornell, and Niels Gyde for their imaginative layouts and stimulating creativity. Also, our artwork assistants, Francesca Gironi and Elisa Pasqualini, for their dedicated work.

The publishers would like to thank the following illustrators: Roberto Battestini; Barbara Bonci; Luisa Cittone: Moreno Chiacchiera; Giovanni Da Re; Pietro Dichiara; Kelly Dyson; Michele Farella; Sergio Giantomassi; Giovanni Giorgi Pierfranceschi; Courtney Huddleston; Pierluigi Longo; Piet Luthi; J.T. Morrow; Asia Nicitto; Dorothy Reinhardt; Giovanni Rolandi; Francesca Scarponi; Lucilla Stellato; Neil Stewart; Jeffrey Thompson; Patrick Welsh.

The publishers would like to thank the following for their kind permission to reproduce the following photographs and other copyright material:

**Student's Book**
**Alamy** p7, p21, p29, p44, p58, p65 (CD: Food Icons); **Associated Press** p10 (Alex Rodriguez); **Dr. Eric H. Chudler, Neuroscience for kids** (http://facultywashington.edu/chudler/neurock.html) p48; **Dreamstime** p8 (Jackie), p18 (Rebecca), p28 (Internet Search Engine), p32 (girl), p56 (Hiroto), p66 (Sunil), p78 (girl); **Günter Gerngross** p49 (sleeping lions); **Hebert Puchta** p49 (leopard); **Helbling Languages** p14 (pizza; hamburger; chair); **©iStockphoto.com** p7 (two boys talking), p8, p11, p12, p14, p15, p18, p21 (students walking), p28, p29 (Rodeo Drive), p32 (boy), p34, p38 (roller coaster), p45 (greenhouse; elephant; carousel), p49 (dolphins; giraffe), p55 (Maria; Sylvie), p56, p64, p65 (students in class), p66, p75, p78 (boy); **Jupiterimages** p38 (Atlanta); **Photos.com** p14 (school bus), p38 (Raleigh; Washington D.C.), p46, p72, p75 (Christina); **Shutterstock** p8 (Simon; Ritu), p10 (Jennifer Lopez), p14 (football), p18 (Ronin), p45 (panda bear; kids), p49 (brown bat), p64 (girl on bike), p65 (vegetables), p68, p69.

The publisher would like to thank the following for their assistance with commissioned photographs: Ed-imaging pp 20, 21, 30, 40, 50, 60, 70; Studio Antonietti p 36.

**Workbook**
**Alamy** p26 (CD: Food Icons), p61; **Dreamstime** p25, p31 (Harry; Sharon); **©iStockphoto.com** p24, p25 (Rio de Janeiro; Brazilian flag), p31 (Jenny); **Photos.com** p25 (Statue of Liberty); **Shutterstock** p12, p18, p25 (Brad Pitt; girl; American flag), p26 (hamburger).

Page numbers refer to the original version.

Every effort has been made to trace the owners of any copyright material in this book. If notified, the publisher will be pleased to rectify any errors or omissions.

| | Grammar | Language Focus and Vocabulary | Skills | MORE! |
|---|---|---|---|---|
| **STARTER SECTION** | • subject pronouns<br>• simple present of *be*<br>• possessive adjectives<br>• plural nouns | • classroom objects and language<br>• greetings<br>• saying hello<br>• numbers<br>• asking about age<br>• international words<br>• colors<br>• days of the week<br><br>**Sounds right**<br>the alphabet | • listen to and understand international words<br>• talk about favorite foods<br>• listen to and complete a dialogue to introduce yourself<br>• read about other people and where they are from<br>• listen to and complete facts about other people<br>• spelling<br>• talk about myself and others<br>**A Song 4 U** *Alphabet stars* | **Check your progress**<br>Starter section |
| **UNIT 1**<br>Hello! | • simple present of *be*<br>• questions with *Who?*<br>• possessive adjectives (review) | • feelings<br><br>**Sounds right**<br>days of the week | • say hello/introduce yourself<br>• ask how people feel<br>• read and write about days of the week and feelings<br>**A Song 4 U** *The weekend is for me* | **Learn MORE through English**<br>Information Technology |
| **UNIT 2**<br>In the classroom | • imperatives<br>• questions with *Who, Where, Why, What, What color?*<br>• prepositions | • classroom objects<br><br>**Sounds right**<br>/ə/ | • ask and say where things are<br>• listen to and understand imperatives<br>• write about your desk | **Check your progress**<br>Units 1 and 2<br><br>**Learn MORE about culture**<br>The East Coast of the U.S.<br><br>**Read MORE for pleasure**<br>A relaxing weekend? |
| **UNIT 3**<br>My bedroom | • *There is/are*<br>• possessive *'s*<br>• adjectives | • furniture<br>• rooms in the house | • describe rooms and furniture<br>• listen to information about a zoo<br>• read a story<br>• write about your ideal room | **Learn MORE through English**<br>Sleep |
| **UNIT 4**<br>Who's that boy? | • *have/has*<br>• the indefinite article | • parts of the body<br>• countries and nationalities<br><br>**Sounds right**<br>/h/ | • talk about nationality<br>• describe people<br>• talk about possessions<br>• listen to and understand physical descriptions<br>• read descriptions of people<br>• write a description of yourself or a friend | **Check your progress**<br>Units 3 and 4<br><br>**Learn MORE about culture**<br>School in the U.S.<br><br>**Read MORE for pleasure**<br>The wide-mouthed frog |
| **UNIT 5**<br>What's for lunch? | • simple present (affirmative)<br>• spelling: third-person singular<br>• adverbs of frequency | • food<br><br>**Sounds right**<br>question intonation | • make and reply to offers and requests<br>• talk about what you eat<br>• read about different diets and foods<br>• listen and complete a dialogue about food<br>• write about your eating habits | **Learn MORE through English**<br>Food from around the world |
| **UNIT 6**<br>Time for a change | • simple present (negatives, questions, and short answers)<br>• object pronouns | • daily activities | • ask and tell the time<br>• talk about daily routines<br>• read about other people's routines<br>• write about your day<br>**A Song 4 U**<br>*The master of time* | **Check your progress**<br>Units 5 and 6<br><br>**Learn MORE about culture**<br>Multicultural America<br><br>**Read MORE for pleasure**<br>The world's best detective |

Wordlist page 120

MAP OF THE BOOK 3

# STARTER SECTION

## Vocabulary  The classroom

**1** Look at the picture. Write the number of the objects.

- ☐ teacher
- ☐ student
- ☐ desk
- ☐ backpack
- ☐ board
- ☐ chair
- ☐ book
- ☐ pencil
- ☐ paper
- ☐ ruler
- ☐ workbook
- ☐ pen
- ☐ eraser
- ☐ pencil case
- ☐ computer

**2** Listen to the sentences. How do you say them in your language?

I don't understand.

Can you repeat that, please?

What's our homework?

Can you spell *pen*, please?

Listen to the CD.

Do exercise 3.

Look at the board.

Copy the sentences.

## Get talking  Greetings

**3** Match the greetings to the correct picture. Write the number. Then listen and write the expressions under the pictures.

- [ ] Good evening.
- [ ] Good morning, Mrs. Jones.
- [ ] Goodbye, Mom.
- [ ] Good morning, Luke.
- [ ] Good afternoon, Mrs. Jones.
- [ ] Good night, Luke.
- [ ] Good night, Mom.
- [ ] Good afternoon, Luke.
- [ ] Goodbye, Luke.
- [ ] Hi, Luke.
- [ ] Hello, Jenny.

1 ...................................................
2 ...................................................
3 ...................................................
4 ...................................................
5 ...................................................
6 ...................................................
7 ...................................................
8 ...................................................
9 ...................................................
10 ...................................................
11 ...................................................

6  STARTER SECTION

## Get talking  Saying hello

**4** Listen and repeat the dialogues.

**Angie**  Hi, Miyu. How are you?
**Miyu**  Hello, Angie. I'm fine. And you?
**Angie**  Great, thanks.

**Ahmed**  Hello, Mark. How are you?
**Mark**  I'm fine. How are you, Ahmed?
**Ahmed**  I'm fine, thanks.

**5** Listen and complete the dialogues.

**Dialogue 1**
**Abi**  Hi, José. ¹............ are you?
**José**  I'm fine, thanks, Abi. And ²............?
**Abi**  I'm OK, thanks.

**Dialogue 2**
**Tina**  Hi, Jana. How ³............ you?
**Jana**  Hello, Tina. ⁴............ fine, thanks. And you?
**Tina**  Great, thanks.

**6** Now practice the dialogues with a partner.

## Vocabulary Numbers

6 **1 Listen and write the numbers.**

six
eight
seventeen
twelve
fifteen
~~two~~

| 1 | 2 | 3 | 4 | 5 | 6 | 7 |
|---|---|---|---|---|---|---|
| one | ......two...... | three | four | five | ...................... | seven |
| **8** | **9** | **10** | **11** | **12** | **13** | **14** |
| ...................... | nine | ten | eleven | ...................... | thirteen | fourteen |
| **15** | **16** | **17** | **18** | **19** | **20** | **21** |
| ...................... | sixteen | ...................... | eighteen | nineteen | twenty | twenty-one |

7 **2 Listen and complete.**

**Sonia** What's your name?
**Jackie** I'm Jackie.
**Sonia** How old are you?
**Jackie** I'm [1]...................... .
**Sonia** Oh, I'm [2]...................... . What's his name?
**Jackie** Mike.
**Sonia** How old is he?
**Jackie** He's [3]...................... .

## Get talking Asking about age

**3 Look at the photos and the names and ages. Close your books and ask and answer with a partner.**

**A** How old is Mike?
**B** He's 12.
**A** That's right. / That's wrong – he's ...

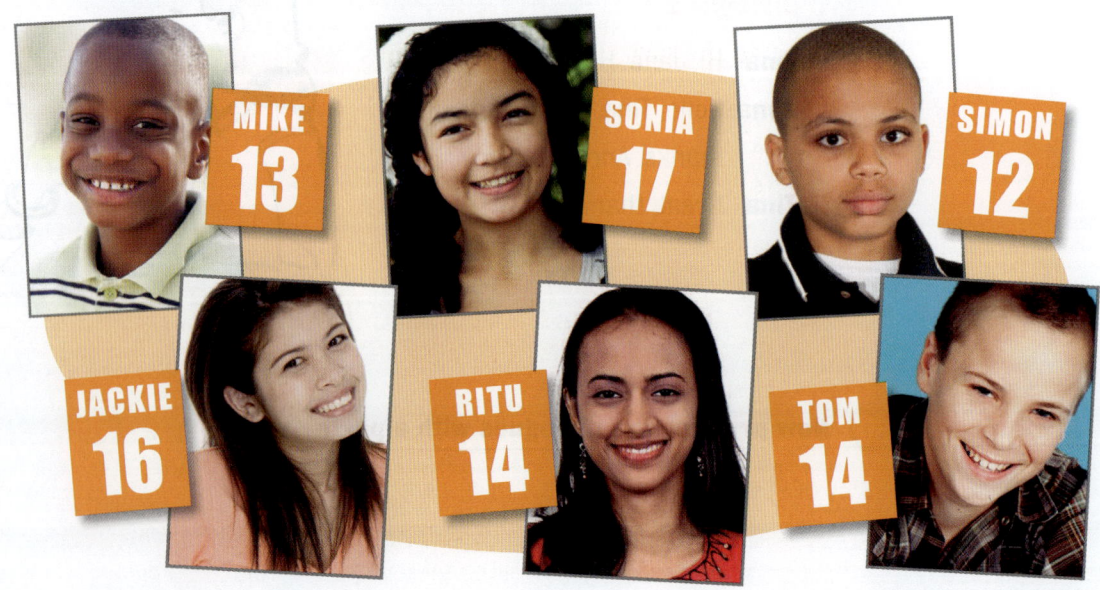

MIKE 13
SONIA 17
SIMON 12
JACKIE 16
RITU 14
TOM 14

## Subject pronouns Singular

| Liam | Hi! **I**'m Liam. |
| Mrs. Wade | How old are **you**, Liam? |
| Liam | **I**'m 13. |
| Mrs. Wade | And your friends? |
| Liam | Kylie. **She**'s 14. Pablo. **He**'s 13. |
| Mrs. Wade | And your pet? |
| Liam | My turtle? **It**'s 135! |

**1** How do you say these words in your language?

1  I  ....................  3  He  ....................  5  It  ....................
2  You  ....................  4  She  ....................

**2** Write the correct pronoun.

1  You  2  ....................  3  ....................  4  ....................  5  ....................

## Simple present of *be* Singular, affirmative

**3** Use the dialogue above to complete the table.

| I | am |  | I'¹........... |  |
| You | are |  | You're |  |
| He |  | 14. | He²........... | 14. |
| She | is |  | She³........... |  |
| It |  |  | It⁴........... |  |

**4** Rewrite the sentences. Use the short form.

1  I am Spanish.   *I'm Spanish.*      4  He is scared.   ....................
2  She is nice.    ....................   5  You are friendly. ....................
3  It is late.     ....................

**5** Complete the sentences with the correct short form.

1  Hello. I ...... Stefan.
2  It ...... a dog.
3  Mark is my friend. He ...... 13.
4  This is Nicole. She ...... nice!
5  Hello, Tom! You ...... late!

## Possessive adjectives Singular

**My** name's Nicole.  **Her** name's Bess.  What's **its** job?
What's **your** name?  What's **his** name?

**6** Use the grammar box above to complete the table.

| Subject pronoun | I | you | he | she | it |
|---|---|---|---|---|---|
| Possessive adjective | ¹ my | ² ......... | ³ ......... | ⁴ ......... | ⁵ ......... |

**7** Complete the sentences. Use *my, your, his,* or *her.*

1  .............. name's Alex Rodriguez.

2  Hi! I'm Steve. What's .............. name?

3  .............. name's Jennifer Lopez.

4  .............. name's José.

**8** Circle the correct word.

1  Hi, *I / my* name is Kevin.
2  *She / Her* is 15.
3  What's *you / your* name?
4  Dawn is *she / her* friend.
5  *He / His* is friendly.
6  *I / My* am scared.

**9** Match the questions and the answers.

1  What's your name?           A  I'm 14.
2  How old are you?            B  My favorite teacher is Mr. Glass.
3  Who is your favorite teacher?  C  My name's Liz.
4  Who is your best friend?    D  My best friend is Olivia.
5  How old is your best friend?  E  She's 13.

**10** Write your own answers to the questions in Exercise 9.
Then ask and answer with a partner.

## Listening

**1** Listen and write the numbers. Then write the correct word under the pictures.

yogurt
hamburgers
hot dogs
apples
pizza

..........................

..........................

..........................

..........................

..........................

## Speaking

**2** Listen and repeat. Then practice other dialogues with a partner.

What's your favorite food? / Apples.

## Listening

**3** Listen to the interview and complete the dialogue.

**Interviewer** What's ¹......................... name?
**Girl** Kristy.
**Interviewer** Where are ².......................... from?
**Girl** I'm from Arizona.
**Interviewer** How old ³.......................... you?
**Girl** I'm 13.
**Interviewer** What's ⁴.......................... favorite food?
**Girl** Hamburgers.
**Interviewer** What's ⁵.......................... favorite number?
**Girl** ⁶.......................... seven.

## Reading

**4** **Read and complete.**

Hi, my name's Michael and I'm from Michigan. I'm 14. My dog's name is Leo and my cat's name is Maggie. They're nice. My favorite food is fruit, and my favorite number is 10.

Hello, I'm Anna and I come from Denver, in Colorado. I'm 15 years old, and 15 is my favorite number! My favorite food is chicken—it's great! My pets are Peter, my hamster, and Piri, my dog.

1  *Michael* is 14.
2  ..................... is 15.
3  Michael is from ..................... .
4  ..................... is from Colorado.
5  Michael's favorite ..................... is 10.
6  Anna's favorite food is ..................... .
7  Leo is a ..................... .
8  Peter is a ..................... .

## Listening

**5** **Listen and complete the table.**

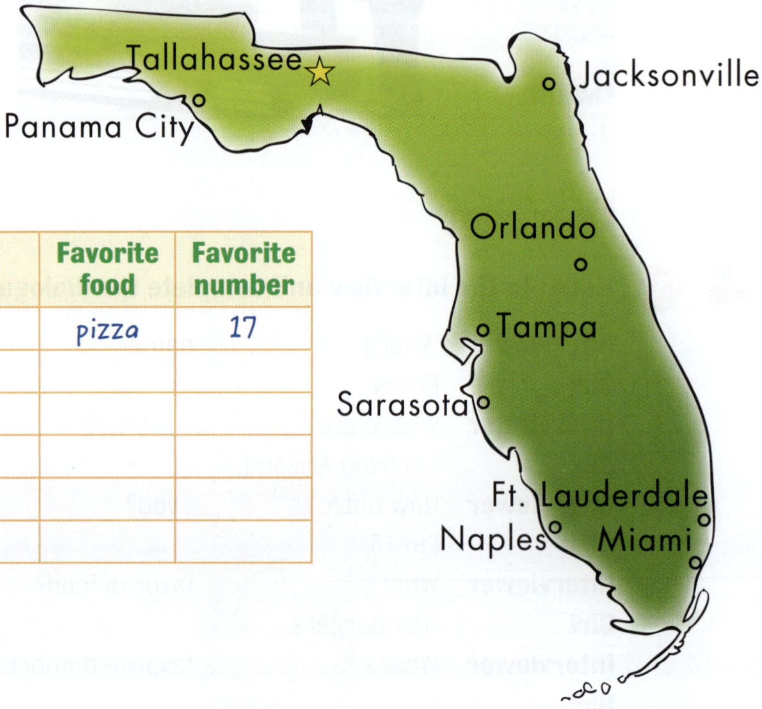

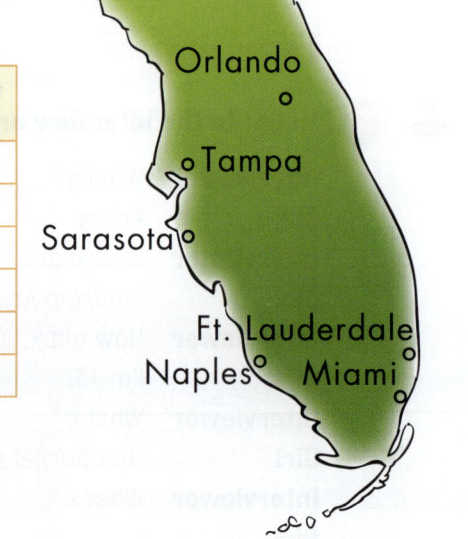

|  | City | Age | Favorite food | Favorite number |
|---|---|---|---|---|
| Alice | Miami | 13 | pizza | 17 |
| Ben |  |  |  |  |
| Karen |  |  |  |  |
| Christopher |  |  |  |  |
| Emily |  |  |  |  |
| Joshua |  |  |  |  |

12 STARTER SECTION

## A Song 4 U  Alphabet stars

**12** **6** Listen and sing.

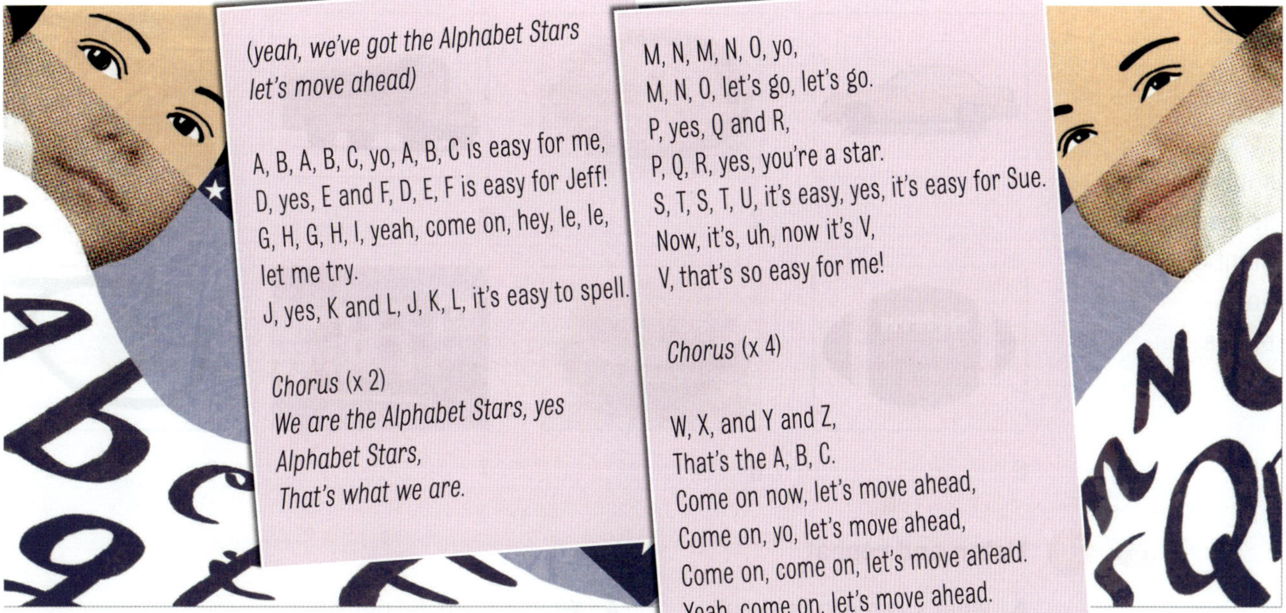

(yeah, we've got the Alphabet Stars
let's move ahead)

A, B, A, B, C, yo, A, B, C is easy for me,
D, yes, E and F, D, E, F is easy for Jeff!
G, H, G, H, I, yeah, come on, hey, le, le,
let me try.
J, yes, K and L, J, K, L, it's easy to spell.

Chorus (x 2)
We are the Alphabet Stars, yes
Alphabet Stars,
That's what we are.

M, N, M, N, O, yo,
M, N, O, let's go, let's go.
P, yes, Q and R,
P, Q, R, yes, you're a star.
S, T, S, T, U, it's easy, yes, it's easy for Sue.
Now, it's, uh, now it's V,
V, that's so easy for me!

Chorus (x 4)

W, X, and Y and Z,
That's the A, B, C.
Come on now, let's move ahead,
Come on, yo, let's move ahead,
Come on, come on, let's move ahead.
Yeah, come on, let's move ahead.

## Sounds right  The alphabet

**13** **7** Listen and repeat. Which four letters are missing?

1  A H J K
2  B C D E P T V
3  F L M N S X
4  Q U W
5  I Y

## Get talking  Spelling

**14** **8** Listen and repeat the dialogue. Then work with a partner and practice dialogues with other names.

## International words

**9** Write the words under the pictures.

taxi
pizza
school bus
supermarket
soccer ball
hamburger
hotel
tennis

1 ....................  2 ....................  3 ....................  4 ....................

5 ....................  6 ....................  7 ....................  8 ....................

**10** Listen and repeat.

A What's *règle* in English?
B It's "ruler."
A Yes, that's right.

A What's *stylo* in English?
B It's "desk."
A No, that's wrong.

**11** Work with a partner. Ask and answer questions about these objects. Use the dialogue from Exercise 10.

What's spaghetti in Italian?

!!!

STARTER SECTION

## Vocabulary  Colors

**12** Listen and write the numbers.

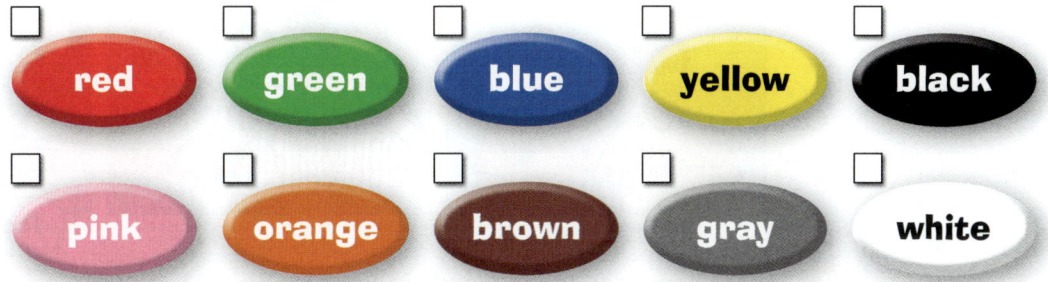

## Vocabulary  Days of the week

**13** Put the days of the week in order using the numbers 1–7. Listen and check.

## Get talking  Saying the days of the week and colors

**14** Work with a partner. Ask and answer.

A What color is Friday?
B Blue.
A Yes!
B What day is red?

## Subject pronouns Plural and singular

1. **How do you say these words in your language?**

   1  We ........................  2  You ........................  3  They ........................

2. **Write the correct subject pronoun.**

## Simple present of *be* Plural, affirmative

3. **Use the cartoon in Exercise 1 to complete the table.**

| Full form | | | Short form | |
|---|---|---|---|---|
| We | **are** | | We[1]............ | |
| You | **are** | friendly. | You[2]............ | friendly. |
| They | **are** | | They[3]............ | |

4. **Rewrite the sentences. Use the short form.**

   1  They are nice.        *They're nice.*        4  She is Canadian.   ........................
   2  You are my friend.   ........................   5  He is Steve.        ........................
   3  We are from London. ........................   6  I am from New York. ........................

5. **Write the correct short form: 'm, 're, or 's.**

1 They ........ from New York.   2 We ........ 14!   3 They ........ my books.   4 I ........ Mexican.   5 He ........ American.

## Possessive adjectives Plural and singular

**Sasha** Hi Jane! Hi David! Is this **your** dog?
**Jane and David** Yes, it's **our** dog?
**Sasha** And is that **your** cat?
**Jane and David** No, it's **their** cat.
**Mia and Chloe** Yes, it's **our** cat.

**6** Use the dialogue above to complete the table.

| Subject pronoun | we | you | they |
|---|---|---|---|
| Possessive adjective | ¹............ | ² *your* | ³............ |

**7** Write *our*, *my*, *their*, *your*, *his*, or *her* under the pictures.

1 Are they ............ hot dogs?

2 She's Maria. ............ house is nice!

3 They're Taylor and Max. And that's ............ dog!

4 This is ............ house.

5 I'm Marta and she's Alice. She's ............ friend!

6 What's ............ name?

## Plural nouns

**8** Look at the box and complete the rule.

| Singular | Plural |
|---|---|
| He is my friend. | They are my friend**s**. |
| Bess is a dog. | Bess and Baron are dog**s**. |

* To make nouns plural, add ¹............
* Some plurals are irregular:

  one child — two **children**   one woman — two **women**
  one man — two **men**   one person — two **people**

**9** Make the sentences plural.

1 The house is nice.
   *The houses are nice.*
2 The man is American.
   ............................
3 Your horse is beautiful.
   ............................
4 My friend is from New York.
   ............................

## Get talking  Talking about myself and others

**10** Listen and make a check next to the sentences the people say.

**1**
- ☐ I'm Rebecca.
- ☐ I'm Veronica.
- ☐ I'm from Philadelphia.
- ☐ I'm from Los Angeles.
- ☐ I'm 14.
- ☐ I'm 15.
- ☐ I'm in ninth grade.
- ☐ I'm in tenth grade.

**2**
- ☐ I'm Ronin.
- ☐ I'm Roger.
- ☐ I'm from Tokyo.
- ☐ I'm from Chicago.
- ☐ I'm 14.
- ☐ I'm 16.
- ☐ I'm in ninth grade.
- ☐ I'm in tenth grade.

**3**
- ☐ We're Sam and Catherine.
- ☐ We're Justin and Jayden.
- ☐ We're from Denver.
- ☐ We're from Orlando.
- ☐ We're 14.
- ☐ We're 16.
- ☐ We're in ninth grade.
- ☐ We're in tenth grade.

**4**
- ☐ We're Helen and Michael.
- ☐ We're Hannah and Bill.
- ☐ We're from Portland.
- ☐ We're from Buenos Aires.
- ☐ We're 14.
- ☐ We're 13.
- ☐ We're in ninth grade.
- ☐ We're in eighth grade.

**11** Talk about the boys and girls from Exercise 10.

1  Veronica's from ................................ . She's ................................ . She's in ................................ .
2  ................................ from ................................ . He's ................................ . He's in ................................ .
3  ................................ and ................................ 're from ................................ . They're ................................ . They're in ................................ .
4  ................................ and ................................ 're from ................................ . They're ................................ . They're in ................................ .

**12** Talk about yourself.

I'm ................................................................
I'm from ........................................................
I'm ................................................................
I'm in ............................................................

STARTER SECTION

# Check your progress Starter Section

**1** Complete the classroom words.

1 t _ _ _ _ _ r
2 d _ _ k
3 r _ l _ r
4 p _ n
5 e _ as _ r
6 s _ _ _ _ _ t
7 p _ _ _ _ l c _ _ e
8 p _ _ _ r
9 b _ _ k
10 ch _ _ r

☐ 10

**2** Match the words to the correct numbers.

1 fifteen          a  18
2 twenty-one       b  16
3 nineteen         c  15
4 eight            d  21
5 sixteen          e  19
6 eighteen         f  8

☐ 6

**3** Complete the sentences with the correct short form of *be*.

1 She ................ American.
2 They ................ from Brazil.
3 We ................ 20.
4 He ................ friendly.
5 I ................ from Michigan.
6 You ................ 13.

☐ 6

**4** Complete the dialogue.

A  ¹................ afternoon, Mrs. Carter.
B  Hello, Tim. How ²................ ³................ ?
A  ⁴................ fine, thanks. And ⁵................ ?
B  Great ⁶................ .

☐ 6

**5** Circle the correct answer.

1 Her name's Rosa. *She / Her* is Brazilian.
2 This is my dog. It *is / are* friendly.
3 We *is / are* from Mexico.
4 Rob and Dan are from Indiana. *They / We* are in class 8A.
5 I love sports. *My / His* favorite sport is football.
6 We're Canadian, but *our / your* favorite food is burritos!

☐ 6

**6** Write the plural form of these words.

1 child    ................
2 man      ................
3 woman    ................
4 person   ................
5 house    ................
6 friend   ................

☐ 6

**7** Complete the names of the days of the week.

1 S _ _ _ _ _ _ _
2 M _ _ _ _ _
3 F _ _ _ _ _
4 T _ _ _ _ _ _ _
5 S _ _ _ _ _
6 T _ _ _ _ _ _

☐ 6

**8** Complete the sentences.

1 They're Emma and Sarah. That's ................ house.
2 We're Paul and Jaime. ................ school is there.
3 You're from Argentina. Are they ................ backpacks?
4 They're American. That's ................ car.

☐ 4

TOTAL ☐ 50

**My progress so far is …**

☺ great!  ☐
😐 good.   ☐
☹ poor.   ☐

STARTER SECTION 19

# UNIT 1 Hello!

### In this unit

**You learn**
- simple present of *be*
- questions with *Who*
- possessive adjectives
- words for feelings

**and then you can**
- say hello/introduce yourself
- ask how people feel

**1  Listen and read.**

| | | | |
|---|---|---|---|
| **Kate** | Hi, Steve. | **Steve** | Oh, sorry. This is my friend Nicole. She plays the flute. |
| **Steve** | Hello, Kate. How are you? | **Kate** | Hello, Nicole. |
| **Kate** | I'm pretty good, thanks. And you? | **Nicole** | Hi, Kate. |
| **Steve** | I'm good. Are you in the band? | **Steve** | And this is my friend Jack. He's a drummer like me. |
| **Kate** | Yes. I'm in the band. I play the clarinet. And who are they? | **Kate** | Hello, Jack. It's nice to meet you. |
| | | **Jack** | It's nice to meet you, too, Kate. |

**2** Write the names under the pictures.

Kate
Nicole
Jack
Steve

1 Steve
2 ............
3 ............
4 ............

**3** Write the names in the spaces.

1 .............................. is pretty good.
2 .............................. is a clarinet player.
3 .............................. is a flute player.
4 .............................. play the drums.

## Get talking  Saying hello / introducing others

**4** Listen and complete the dialogues.

**Dialogue 1**

**Olivia**  Hello, Emma. How are you?
**Emma**  Hi, Olivia. I'm fine, thanks. How ¹.............. you?
**Olivia**  Great, thanks.
**Emma**  Olivia, this ².............. Carl. Carl, this ³.............. Olivia.
**Carl**  Hi, Olivia. Nice to meet you.
**Olivia**  Hi, Carl. Nice to meet you, too.

**Dialogue 2**

**Noah**  Hi, Anna. Meet Michael and Tony. They ⁴.............. new here.
**Michael**  Hi, Anna.
**Anna**  Hi, Michael.
**Tony**  Hello, Anna. How ⁵.............. you?
**Anna**  Hi, Tony. I'm fine, thanks. And ⁶..............?
**Michael**  I'm OK, thank you.
**Anna**  Oh, sorry. I ⁷.............. late. Bye!
**Michael and Tony**  Bye, Anna.
**Noah**  Bye!

**5** Act out dialogues in class. Use your own names.

UNIT 1  21

# Language Focus

### Vocabulary Feelings

**1** Follow the lines, and ask and answer questions.

happy
angry
excited
sad
cold
bored
hungry
hot
scared
nervous

**A** Who's happy?

**B** John. Who's…?

### Get talking Asking how people feel

**2** Work with a partner. Look at the pictures, close your book and ask and answer.

**A** What's wrong with Victor?

**B** He's tired. What's wrong with Sally and Liz?

**A** They're scared.

# Grammar

## Simple present of *be* Affirmative

**I'm** in the band.
**He's** (**She's**/**It's**) OK.
**We're** (**You're**/**They're**) good.

I'm = I am

He's/She's/It's = He is/She is/It is

We're /You're/They're = We are/
You are/They are

**1** Complete the sentences with *'m*, *'re*, or *'s*.

1 This is Katie. She ………… from Texas.
2 I ………… Victoria, not Vicky.
3 We ………… hungry.
4 Sandy and Jolyn, you ………… late!
5 Meet Brandon and Morgan. They ………… new here.
6 Thank you, Jane. You ………… great!
7 It ………… a nice dog!
8 Isabel, meet Dominic. He ………… my friend.

## Simple present of *be* Negative

**I'm not** from Texas.
**You/We/They aren't** new here.
**He/She/It isn't** OK.

**2** Rewrite the sentences. Use the short form.

1 It is not cold. *It isn't cold.*
2 We are not Texan.
   ……………………………………
3 You are not late.
   ……………………………………
4 I am not angry.
   ……………………………………
5 She is not happy.
   ……………………………………
6 They are not friendly.
   ……………………………………

**3** Complete the sentences. Use the short form.

1 It *isn't* a dog. It's a cat!
2 They ……………… Texan. They're New Yorkers.
3 He ……………… angry. He's hungry.
4 You ……………… right. You're wrong.
5 She ……………… Ana. She's Lydia!
6 We ……………… 13. We're 14.
7 It ……………… my dog. It's his dog.
8 I ……………… Steve. I'm Matteo.

## Simple present of *be* Questions and short answers

**Am I** scared of dogs?
Yes, **you are.** | No, **you aren't.**

**Are you** OK?
Yes, **I am.** | No, **I'm not.**

**Is he**/**she**/**it** friendly?
Yes, **he/she/it is.** | No, **he/she/it isn't.**

**Are we/you/they** new here?
Yes, **we/you/they are.** | No, **we/you/they aren't.**

**4** Complete the questions and short answers.

1 *Is* Ana Texan?        No, she *isn't* .
2 ………… you bored?        Yes, I ………… .
3 ………… I right?          No, you ………… .
4 ………… it a cat?         Yes, it ………… .
5 ………… they excited?     Yes, ………… ………… .
6 ………… we wrong?         No, ………… ………… .
7 ………… Steve 16?         No, ………… ………… .
8 ………… you hot?          No, ………… ………… .

## Questions with Who...?

A **Who's** he?
B Santiago. He's from Argentina.

A **Who are** they?
B Pablo and Maria. They're from Mexico.

How do you say *Who…?* in your language?

5  **Write the questions.**

1  *Who's she* ?
   She's Ana.
2  ………………………………………?
   He's my friend, Steve.
3  ………………………………………?
   They're Steve and Lydia.
4  ………………………………………?
   I'm Sarah Jones.
5  ………………………………………?
   We're Mike and Jenny Smith.
6  ………………………………………?
   She's the new teacher.
7  ………………………………………?
   My favorite band is the Jonas Brothers.
8  ………………………………………?
   He's our friend Tony.

## Possessive adjectives  Review

I'm Peter. This is **my** friend Tom.
Lily, is this **your** dog?
This is my friend. **His** name's Mike.
Meet Lydia and **her** friend Steve.
It's a nice dog. What's **its** name?
We're happy. **Our** favorite band's in town!
Girls and boys, I'm **your** new English teacher.
Meet Jane and James and **their** friends from Michigan.

6 **Listen and repeat the rap.**

# Skills

## Reading

**1** Read the story.

**❶** Max is on his new bike. His bike is red. His bike is fast. He's happy.

**❷** Tom's his friend. His bike is fast, too, but he isn't happy. He's nervous. He's very, very nervous!

**❸** Mr. and Mrs. Cross are at the bus stop. They aren't happy. They're cold. They're very, very cold!

**❹** Mrs. Bing is at the café. She isn't happy. She's angry. She's very, very angry!

**❺** The duck's in the road. It isn't happy. It's scared. It's very, very scared!

**❻** Max isn't on his bike now, and he isn't very happy. But the duck's happy and Mrs. Bing is happy. And Mr. and Mrs. Cross are happy. And Tom's happy, too. They're all happy. They're all very, very happy!

**2** Complete the table.

|  | In Picture | In Picture |
|---|---|---|
| Max | 1: *is very happy* | 6: *isn't very happy* |
| Tom | 2: | 6: |
| Mr. and Mrs. Cross | 3: | 6: |
| Mrs. Bing | 4: | 6: |
| the duck | 5: | 6: |

UNIT 1

**3** Work with a partner. Read the dialogue and draw an expression on the faces of Maria and Ella. Create other dialogues and expressions for Tim, Fred, and Lucas.

A  Is Ella happy?
B  No, she isn't.
   She's sad.
   Is Maria happy?
A  Yes, she is.

## Sounds right  Days of the week

**4** Listen and repeat.

Monday, Tuesday, Wednesday—sad!
Thursday, Friday—they aren't bad!
Saturday and Sunday—great!
Tomorrow's Monday—don't be late!

## Reading

**5** Read the sentences and write the day of the week above the picture.

It's Monday morning.
Sue's tired.

It's Tuesday evening.
Sue's bored.

It's Wednesday afternoon.
Sue's angry.

It's Thursday morning.
Sue's nervous.

It's Friday afternoon.
Sue's excited. Tomorrow's
the weekend.

It's Saturday afternoon.
Sue's busy. She's shopping.

It's Sunday. Sue's happy.

## A Song 4 U  The weekend is for me

**6** Listen and complete. Then sing.

excited (x 2)   nervous (x 2)
bored (x 2)   angry (x 2)
tired (x 2)

On Monday I'm so ¹.........,
as ²......... as I can be.
I really don't like Monday,
no, Monday's not for me.
(*No, it's not, not for me.*)

On Tuesday I'm so ³........., yeah,
as ⁴......... as I can be.
There's nothing good on TV,
no, Tuesday's not for me.
(*No, it's not, not for me.*)

*Chorus*
*It's just another day,
another day, you see.
It's a day like many others,
it's just not good, not good
for me.*

On Wednesday I'm so ⁵.........,
as ⁶......... as I can be.
I've got a lot of homework,
no, Wednesday's not for me.
(*No, it's not, not for me.*)

On Thursday I'm so ⁷.........,
as ⁸......... as I can be.
We have a test on Thursday,
no, Thursday's not for me.
(*No, it's not, not for me.*)
*Chorus*

On Friday I'm ⁹.........,
as ¹⁰......... as I can be.
Tomorrow is the weekend,
the weekend is for me.

*The weekend's here,
the weekend's here, you see.
The weekend is fantastic,
it's just the best for me!
The weekend is fantastic.
The weekend is for me!* (x 2)

## Writing for your Portfolio

**7** How do you feel during the week? Write a short description.

On Monday I'm not tired. I'm excited...

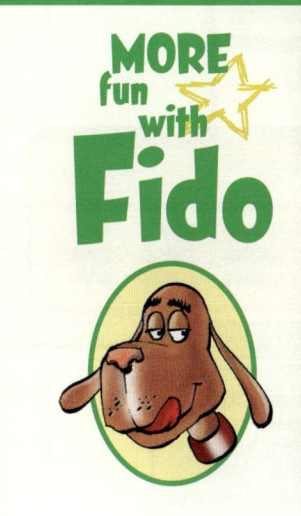

UNIT 1   27

# Information Technology

**Key words**

World Wide Web
Internet research
web page
search engine
search for
type
select
click on
webquest
download

## FACT FILE

- There are billions of pages on the web. At the moment, English is the main language on the web.
- Google and Yahoo are two very popular search engines.
- To search for pictures only, go to www.google.com and click on *images*.

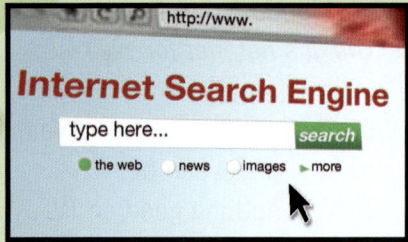

Then type a word, such as *Rockies*. A second later you have a lot of beautiful pictures.

- When you use Google, these tricks help you find information.

| You type: | You find: |
|---|---|
| New York people | pages with "New York," and "people" |
| New York OR Chicago | pages with "New York," or "Chicago" |
| New York -people | pages with "New York" but not "people" |
| "concerts in Chicago" | pages with the exact phrase "concerts in Chicago" |

**1** Read the facts about the *American MORE!* website.

**This is what you find on www.more-online.com/american**

- Fun stories to read
- Interesting interviews and other texts to listen to
- Interactive grammar and vocabulary exercises

**It is easy to find your way around the *American MORE!* website.**

- Go to www.more-online.com/american
- Click on extra resources
- Click on a unit
- Select the activity you want to do

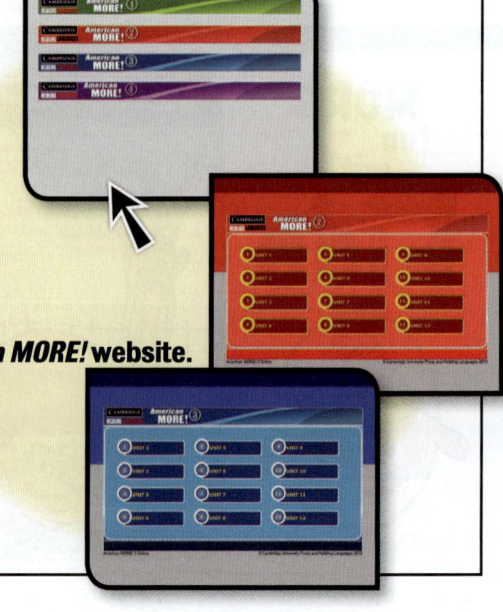

**2** The *American MORE!* webquest. Go to the *American MORE!* website and write the answers to these questions.

1. How many activities are there on the *American MORE!* website for Unit 10?
2. There is a story in Unit 10 called Mrs. Bing's Pet Shop. What is a "snark?"
3. In Unit 6, there is a Listening exercise, The Pirates' Parade. Who is Toby's pet?
4. Which unit has a grammar exercise on time?
5. In Unit 12, what is the Get Talking activity about? Do the activity, and then practice the dialogues with a partner.

## Mini-project

**3** Work in groups. Use the Internet.

1. Find the names of the three biggest cities in the United States.
2. Choose one of these cities. Find three pictures of it. Download the pictures.
3. Find out how many people live in the city.
4. Find the name of a hotel there. Find a picture of it.
5. Find the name of a museum or a school there.
6. Find the name of a baseball team.

**4** Write a report. Include your pictures.

**Report: Our Internet research**
The three biggest cities in the U.S. are New York, Los Angeles, and Chicago.
**The city of our choice:** Los Angeles
**Number of people:** 3.8 million
**Name of a hotel:** The Hollywood Roosevelt
**Baseball team:** The L.A. Dodgers
Here are some more pictures of Los Angeles.

The Hollywood Roosevelt
Dodger Stadium
The Getty Museum
Rodeo Drive

**MORE!** Now you can watch Episode 1 of *The Story of the Stones.*

UNIT 1 29

Information Technology

# UNIT 2 In the classroom

**In this unit**

**You learn**
- imperatives
- questions with *Who, Where, Why, What, What color?*
- words for classroom objects
- prepositions

**and then you can**
- ask and say where things are

### 1  Listen and read.

**Kate**  Nicole, don't sit there. Sit here, next to me.
**Nicole**  OK, Kate. Thanks. What's the matter, Steve?
**Steve**  Where's my pen?
**Nicole**  I don't know. What color is it? Red?
**Steve**  No, it's black.
**Kate**  Look! It's there, on the floor under the table. Pick it up.
**Nicole**  Who's she?
**Kate**  I don't know—maybe she's a new teacher?
**Miss Young**  Good morning. I'm Miss Young, your new teacher.
**Nicole**  Good morning, Miss Young. You're right, Kate!
**Steve**  Good morning.
**Miss Young**  Why are you under the desk?
**Steve**  My pen's on the floor. Ouch!
**Miss Young**  Don't laugh, class—it isn't funny!
**Kate**  Sorry, Miss Young.
**Miss Young**  Well, come out and stand up. Who are you?
**Steve**  Steve, Steve Johnson.
**Miss Young**  Alright, sit down and be quiet. Now, everyone, open your books.

**2** **Circle the correct answer.**

1 Nicole sits next to *Steve* / *Kate* .
2 Steve's pen is *black* / *red* .
3 His pen's on the *floor* / *desk* .
4 Miss Young is a new *student* / *teacher* .
5 Miss Young is *happy* / *upset* when the girls laugh.
6 She tells *Steve* / *everyone* to open *his* / *their* books.

**3** **Complete with *in*, *on*, *under*, *next to*, *in front of,* and *behind*. Then listen and check.**

1  It's ................. the car.   2  It's ................. the car.   3  It's ................. the car.

4  It's ................. the car.   5  It's ................. the car.   6  It's ................. the car.

### Get talking  Saying where things are

**4** **Ask and answer questions about the animals and the cars.**

A  Where's the red car?
B  It's behind the …

A  Where's the white cat?
B  It's …

UNIT 2  31

# Language Focus

## Vocabulary  Classroom objects

**1**  Listen. Are the sentences you hear correct?

Yes!

No, it's ...........

1. CD player
2. board
3. computer
4. door
5. desk
6. floor
7. English book
8. chair
9. window
10. laptop

**2**  Work with a partner. Cover the picture in Exercise 1. Ask and answer questions about the color of the objects.

A What color's the desk?

B It's brown.

## Get talking  Saying where things are

**3**  Draw the objects listed to the left of the picture. Work with a partner and ask and answer questions.

ruler
backback
dictionary
pencil case
pen
eraser

A Where's the ...?

B Is it in/on/under/in front of/next to/behind the ...?

This is my classroom. Isn't it cool?

32 UNIT 2

# Grammar

## Imperatives

**1** Look at the dialogue on page 30 and complete.

**Open** your books.
**Don't** sit there.
1 ........................ up.
2 ........................ it up.
3 ........................ down.
4 ........................ laugh.

**2** Write the phrases from the grammar box in Exercise 1 under the correct picture.

1 Stand up      2 ........................

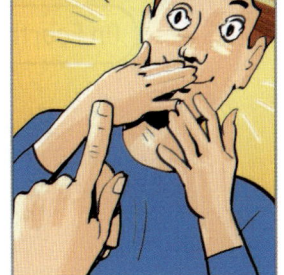

3 ........................    4 ........................

5 ........................    6 ........................

**3** Complete the sentences. Use the verbs listed below.

| open | don't open | look | don't look |
| sit | don't sit | ~~be~~ | don't be |

1 ...Be... quiet!    2 ........................

3 ............... down, please.    4 ........................ it!

5 ................ sad.    6 ........................ there!

7 ........................ it!    8 ........................

UNIT 2 33

## Questions with *Who, Where, Why, What, What color?*

**4** Look at the dialogue on page 30 and fill in the blanks below.

How do you say these question words in your language?

..................'s my pen?
.................. color is it?
..................'s she?
.................. are you under the desk?

**5** Match the questions and answers.

1 Where's Nicole?
2 What's his name?
3 What color's your cat?
4 Who's Miss Young?
5 Why are you happy?

a She's the new teacher.
b Because my friend is here.
c She's in the classroom.
d It's black and white.
e It's Steve.

**6** Complete the questions.

1 *What color's* your bicycle?
It's green.
2 .................. her name?
Sandra.
3 .................. she?
She's my new friend.
4 .................. your dogs?
They're in the house.
5 .................. your favorite food?
It's pizza.
6 .................. your favorite film star?
Matt Damon.
7 .................. your backpack?
Green and blue.
8 .................. she sad?
Because her friends aren't here.

**7** Reorder the words and write questions.

1 from / where / you / are
   *Where are you from* ..................?
2 is / what / favorite / band / your
   ..................?
3 color / are / dogs / what / his
   ..................?
4 house / in / who / is / the
   ..................?
5 Nicole / angry / is / why
   ..................?
6 is / school / where / your
   ..................?
7 their / what / car / color / is
   ..................?
8 teacher / favorite / who / your / is
   ..................?

**8** Ask and answer questions with a partner. Use the question words to help you.

...'s your house?
...'s your best friend?
...'s your favorite color?
... are you from?
... your favorite band?
... your phone number?

On Fourth Street.

34 UNIT 2

# Skills

## Listening

  **Complete the sentences. Then listen and check.**

walk  run  look
wait  open  see
put

1 ............ your books in your backpack.
2 ............ your pencils in your pencil case.
3 ............ to school.

4 ............ at your watch. You're late!
5 ............ to school.
6 ............ the door of your classroom.

7 ............ the classroom is empty.
8 Oh, no! It's Saturday.
9 ............ for your brother to come and get you.

## Sounds right /ə/

  **a Listen and repeat.**

1 teach<u>er</u>  2 op<u>en</u>  3 p<u>a</u>lm  4 pizz<u>a</u>  5 th<u>e</u>  6 <u>a</u>bout

**b Listen and repeat.**

1 Why is the teacher under the desk?
2 What is the book about?

## Speaking

3 Work with a partner. Student A hides an object. Student B guesses where it is.

A Where's my pen?
B Is it in your backpack?
A No, it isn't.
B Is it in your dictionary?
A No, it isn't.
B Is it under your pencil case?
A Yes, it is.

## Writing for your Portfolio

4 Read Nicole's text about her desk. Write a similar text.

My desk is not in order! My blue pen is in my dictionary. My pencil case is on my backpack, and my pencils are on the backpack, too. My English book is behind the computer. My ruler is in my English book. My cat is on the computer! Where is my red pen? No idea!

# Check your progress  Units 1 and 2

**1 Write the classroom objects.**

1  w _ _ _ _ _
2  r _ _ _ _
3  c _ _ _ _ _ _ _
4  CD _ _ _ _ _ _
5  d _ _ _
6  c _ _ _ _

☐ 6

**2 Complete the questions.**

1  ............... you bored?
2  ............... your pen on your desk?
3  ............... Miley Cyrus from New York?
4  ............... Sue and John happy?
5  ............... your father Puerto Rican?
6  ............... our math test tomorrow?

☐ 6

**3 Fill in each of the blanks below with a question number from Exercise 2.**

a  ............... No, she's from Poland.
b  ............... Yes, I am.
c  ............... No, she isn't.
d  ............... No, it's on Tuesday.
e  ............... Yes, it is.
f  ............... Yes, they are.

☐ 6

**4 Reorder the dialogue.**

............... I'm nervous.
............... Hi, Lucy. How are you?
............... Because tomorrow is our math test.
............... Why not? What's wrong?
............... I'm not very happy.
............... Why are you nervous?

☐ 6

**5 Complete the questions and answers.**

1  ............... color is your English book?
   ....................................................
2  ............... is your favorite actor?
   ....................................................
3  ............... is your house?
   ....................................................
4  ............... is your math teacher?
   ....................................................
5  ............... is the capital of Florida?
   ....................................................

☐ 10

**6 Write sentences in the negative form.**

1  I'm American.
   ....................................................
2  They are hungry.
   ....................................................
3  It's very hot today.
   ....................................................
4  My teachers are friendly.
   ....................................................
5  Hamburgers are my favorite food.
   ....................................................
6  We're from Florida.
   ....................................................

☐ 6

**7 Complete the sentences with the correct possessive adjective.**

1  That is Sarah. This is ............... dog.
2  Hi, we're David and Tom. This is ............... house.
3  They are students. That's ............... school.
4  Hi, Tom! Is that ............... dog?
5  What are ............... names?

☐ 5

**8 Translate these phrases into your own language.**

1  Don't sit there.      ...............................
2  Open the window.      ...............................
3  Don't be sad.         ...............................
4  Look there.           ...............................
5  Don't be mad.         ...............................

☐ 5

**TOTAL** ☐ 50

**My progress so far is ...**

☺ great!   ☐
😐 good.   ☐
☹ poor.   ☐

**Learn MORE about culture**

# The East Coast of the U.S.

**1** Match the descriptions to the correct picture. Then write the name of the city.

1. Hi, my name's Emma. I'm from ..................... It is the capital city of the United States. Many tourists come here to see sites like the Washington Monument.
2. Hi, my name's Jake. I'm from ....................., a popular destination in Florida. Here you can find many theme parks.
3. Hello, I'm Melissa. I'm from ....................., the capital city of Georgia. My favorite place is Turner Field. This is where the Atlanta Braves play.
4. Hello, I'm David. I'm from ....................., the capital of North Carolina. My favorite place is the IMAX theater.

## FACT FILE

**REGIONS**
New England, Mid-Atlantic, South Atlantic

**POPULATION**
New England: 14,303,542
Mid Atlantic: 40,621,237
South Atlantic: 58,398,377
(Total 113,323,156)

**STATES**
New England: New Hampshire, Maine, Vermont, Massachusetts, Connecticut, Rhode Island
Mid-Atlantic: New York, Pennsylvania, New Jersey
South Atlantic: Delaware, Maryland, West Virginia, North Carolina, Virginia, South Carolina, Georgia, Florida

a **Raleigh**
b **Washington, D.C.**
c **Orlando**
d **Atlanta**

**2** Listen and complete the table.

|  | NEW ENGLAND | MID-ATLANTIC | SOUTH ATLANTIC |
|---|---|---|---|
| **Mountains** | Mount Washington | 1..................... | Stone Mountain |
| **Rivers** | Connecticut River | Allegheny River | 2..................... River |
| **Lakes** | Lake Champlain | 3..................... | 4..................... |
| **Cities** | Boston | New York City | 5..................... |

Poconos
Savannah
Okeechobee
Finger Lakes
Atlanta

**3** **Over 2 U!** Write a short description of the place where you live.

**MORE!** Now you can watch Episode 2 of *The Story of the Stones*.

# A relaxing weekend?

"I'm SO happy it's Saturday!"

"Time to relax! The weekend!"

"Come on, guys! It's time to go!"

"We're late for dance practice, Mom."

"Don't worry. We're almost there."

"Come on, Karen, hurry up! We're late for soccer!"

"I'm worried. We're late for the game!"

"Are you ok, Jake?"

"I'll just park the car."

"They're very good."

"Sorry you lost!"

"It's ok. We'll win next time!"

"Wow! It's only noon? I'm so tired!"

"Well, I'm not surprised. All you've done is run around!"

Read MORE for pleasure

For **MORE!** Go to www.more-online.com/american for related activities and questions.

UNIT 2  39

# UNIT 3 My bedroom

## In this unit

**You learn**
- *There is/are*
- possessive *'s*
- words for furniture
- adjectives
- rooms in the house

**and then you can**
- describe rooms and furniture

### 1 Listen and read.

**Nicole** What's your new bedroom like, Kate?
**Kate** It's not very big. But it's really nice!
**Steve** Are there any good posters?
**Kate** Yes, a Foo Fighters poster and …
**Jack** Foo Fighters? Who are they?
**Steve** Oh, come on, Jack! They're really famous!
**Kate** And there's a nice big wardrobe, too.
**Jack** Is there a bookshelf?
**Kate** Yes, there is. It's next to the bed. It's small, but there aren't a lot of books in my room!
**Nicole** Is there a light for reading in bed?
**Kate** No, there isn't.
**Steve** What else is there?
**Kate** Well, there are blue curtains, two blue chairs, and a desk. On the desk there's a …
**Jack** Computer?
**Kate** Yes, and there's a DVD player in it!
**Nicole** Great! Can we watch some DVDs at your place?
**Kate** Sure. Let's watch a DVD of the Foo Fighters!
**Steve** OK!

**2** Read the dialogue again and answer *Yes* or *No* to the questions.

1 Is Kate's bedroom big? ...No...
2 Are the Foo Fighters famous? .........
3 Is Kate's bookshelf big? ............
4 Are her curtains green? ............
5 Is there a Foo Fighters' poster in her room? ............
6 Is there a closet in her room? ............
7 Are there a lot of books in her room? ............
8 Is there a DVD player in her computer? ............

## Get talking   Describing things

**3** Find the opposites.

BIG   friendly   good
late   new   old
unfriendly   BAD   early
small

**4** Look at the pictures. Ask and answer questions with a partner.

A Is the house big?
B No, it's very small.

big?     good?    friendly?

new?    early?

UNIT 3   41

# Language Focus

## Vocabulary Furniture

**1** Listen and write the numbers.

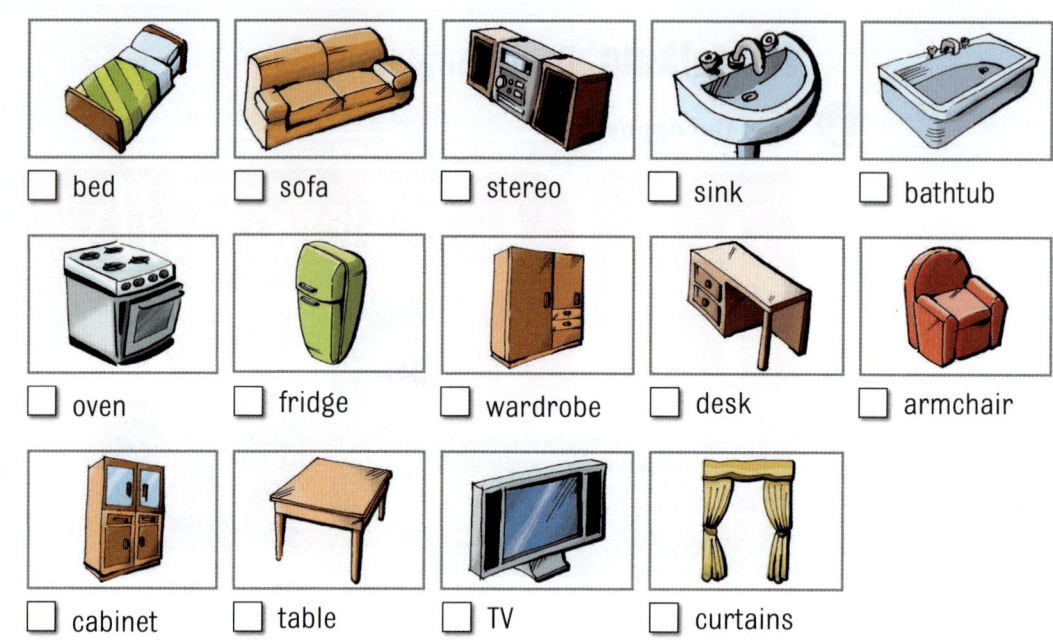

☐ bed  ☐ sofa  ☐ stereo  ☐ sink  ☐ bathtub

☐ oven  ☐ fridge  ☐ wardrobe  ☐ desk  ☐ armchair

☐ cabinet  ☐ table  ☐ TV  ☐ curtains

**2** Look at the house, and then close your books and say what is in each room.

In the living room, there's a TV and ………………… .

In the kitchen, there are two chairs ………………… .

bathroom

Steve's room

bedroom

kitchen

hall

living room

garage

42 UNIT 3

# Grammar

## There is/are

**1** Look at the dialogue on page 40 and complete the table below.

| Affirmative | Negative | Questions | Positive | Negative |
|---|---|---|---|---|
| ¹............ a nice big closet. | There isn't a closet. | ³............ a bookshelf? | Yes, ⁵............ | No, there isn't. |
| ²............ blue curtains. | There aren't curtains. | ⁴............ any good posters? | Yes, there are. | No, there aren't. |

**2** Complete the sentences with *There's* or *There are*.

1. *There's* a desk in my room.
2. ............ green curtains in his room.
3. ............ a ham sandwich on the table.
4. ............ a book on the floor.
5. ............ six children in the room.
6. ............ nice posters in our classroom.
7. ............ a cat on my bed!
8. ............ 22 people in my class.

**3** Complete with the correct form of *there is* or *there are*.

1. *Is there* a TV in your room?
   No, ............ .
2. ............ a car in the garage?
   Yes, ............ .
3. ............ two beds in your room?
   No, ............ .
4. ............ a sofa in your living room?
   No, ............ .
5. ............ a lot of books in your bedroom?
   Yes, ............ .
6. ............ a hallway in your house?
   Yes, ............ .
7. ............ a lot of sandwiches in the kitchen?
   No, ............ .
8. ............ 22 desks in your classroom?
   Yes, ............ .

## Get talking  Describing rooms and furniture

**4** Listen. Which rooms are the people in?

Conversation one: ............
Conversation two: ............
Conversation three: ............
Conversation four: ............

**5** Read the description of Nicole's ideal room.

*In my ideal room, there's a big bed and there are yellow curtains. Yellow is my favorite color. There are a lot of posters of pop stars and horses. There's a nice desk. On the desk, there's a computer with a big screen. There are two chairs and there are a lot of shelves for my books and CDs. There is also a good stereo.*

**6** This is a picture of Nicole's ideal room described in Exercise 5. Find three more errors.

Number 1: The bed is small.

## Possessive 's

Bob**'s** dog. (This is Bob. This is his dog.)

Michelle**'s** pizza. (This is Michelle. This is her pizza.)

**7** Read the sentences and check the correct column. Is the '*s* a possessive or the short form of *is*?

|   | possessive | is |
|---|---|---|
| 1 Where are Steve's DVDs? | ☐ | ☐ |
| 2 He's in the house. | ☐ | ☐ |
| 3 They're Nicole's things. | ☐ | ☐ |
| 4 Who's she? | ☐ | ☐ |
| 5 The teacher's new. | ☐ | ☐ |
| 6 Where are the teacher's books? | ☐ | ☐ |

**8** Rewrite the sentences. Replace the possessive adjectives with a name.

1 It's her desk. (Kate)
  It's Kate's desk.

2 They're his books. (Steve)

3 It's her room. (Nicole)

4 Where's his pen? (Jack)

5 Pizza is her favorite food. (Michelle)

6 What is his favorite color? (Steve)

44 UNIT 3

# Skills

## Listening

**1** Listen to the advertisement for the zoo. Number the sentences in the correct order.

## Come to Maxwell Zoo!

**1** There's a big **greenhouse**!

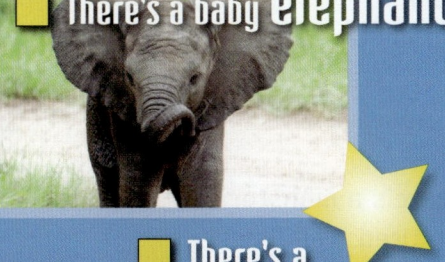

☐ There's a baby **elephant**!

☐ There's a pool with **manatees**.

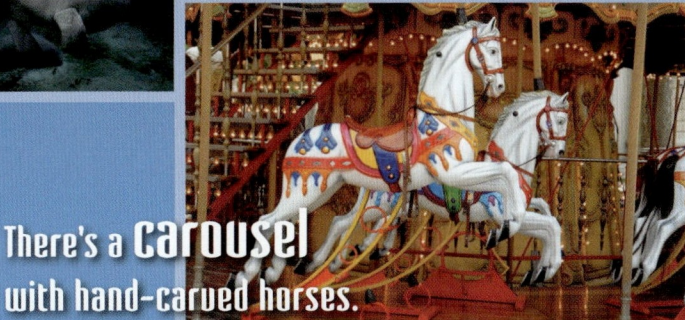

☐ There are **panda bears**.

☐ There's a **carousel** with hand-carved horses.

Ages 10 and up: $10     Ages 2–9: $7     Under 2: Free

## Take the quiz

|  | Yes | No |
|---|---|---|
| There's a gorilla. | ☆ | ☆ |
| There's a baby elephant. | ☆ | ☆ |
| There's a swimming pool for kids. | ☆ | ☆ |
| There are hippo rides. | ☆ | ☆ |
| There's a carousel. | ☆ | ☆ |
| Children under 10 pay $10 to get in. | ☆ | ☆ |

## Reading

**2** Read the text.

**Yosemite National Park** in California is very big. There are more than 3,000 square kilometers of hills, forests, green valleys, and beautiful lakes. There are also a lot of hotels, lodges, and campgrounds.

**Chloe, Harriet, Dean, and Tom are on a school trip in Yosemite. They are at a campsite.**

| | |
|---|---|
| **Tom** | Help! |
| **Dean** | What's the matter? |
| **Tom** | There's a monster in the forest. A monster with six eyes. |
| **Dean** | What? |
| **Tom** | There's a monster with six eyes. |
| **Dean** | I'm tired. Tell Chloe. |

| | |
|---|---|
| **Tom** | Chloe! Chloe! |
| **Chloe** | What's the matter? |
| **Tom** | There's a monster in the forest. A monster with six eyes. |
| **Chloe** | What? |
| **Tom** | There's a monster with six eyes. |
| **Chloe** | Tom, please. I'm tired. Tell Harriet. |

| | |
|---|---|
| **Tom** | Harriet! Harriet! |
| **Harriet** | What's the matter? |
| **Tom** | There's a monster in the forest. A monster with six eyes. |
| **Harriet** | What? |
| **Tom** | There's a monster with six eyes in the forest. |
| **Harriet** | OK, OK. Where's my lantern? |

| | |
|---|---|
| **Harriet** | Where? |
| **Tom** | Over there! A monster with six eyes. |
| **Harriet** | Ah. |
| **Tom** | What is it? |
| **Harriet** | That's the monster! It's amazing. It's three little owls in a tree. |

## 3 Who says what?

- It's amazing.
- There's a monster with six eyes.
- I'm tired. Tell Harriet.

1 ..........................  2 ..........................  3 ..........................

## Speaking

**4** Work with a partner. Complete the dialogue with the phrases below. Then say aloud.

> What else is there?  Is there a bookshelf?
> No, there isn't.  What's your new bedroom like, Kate?

**Tiff** 1 ..........................................................................
**Kate** Well, it's not very big.
**Jack** 2 ..........................................................................
**Kate** Yes, there is. It's small, but that's OK.
**Tiff** Is there a light for reading in bed?
**Kate** 3 ..........................................................................
**Steve** 4 ..........................................................................
**Kate** Well, there are blue curtains and two blue chairs. There's a desk, and on it there's a computer.

## Writing for your Portfolio

**5** Describe your ideal room.

> In my ideal room there is ....
> There are ....

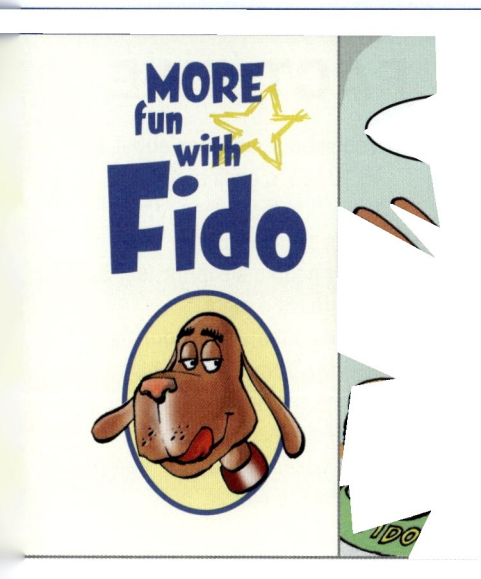

**MORE fun with Fido**

UNIT 3 47

# Sleep

What is sleep? Sleep is the body's natural "pause button." During sleep, the muscles relax. Breathing slows down. The heartbeat slows. The brain works differently, too.

Why do we sleep? Scientists aren't sure. But they are sure that sleep is very important for the brain and the body.

**Key words**
body　scientists
muscles　human
breathing　hibernate
heartbeat　in danger
brain　hunted

## The different stages of sleep—Human (35-year-old)

**1** Read the text. Write the stages of sleep in the correct place on the graph.

Humans sleep in cycles of about 90–120 minutes. There are two kinds of sleep: non-REM (four stages) and REM sleep.

**Stage one**
During this stage of sleep, you are not really asleep. The body slows, the muscles relax. It is easy to wake up from this kind of sleep.

**Stage two**
After 10 minutes of light sleep, you start "true sleep." This lasts about 20 minutes. People breathe more slowly, and the heart beats more slowly. Most sleep in the night is "true sleep."

**Stage three**
Breathing and heartbeat are very slow now.

**REM sleep**
*REM* means "rapid eye movement." This is because the eyes move very quickly. The first rapid eye movement (REM) phase starts about 70 to 90 minutes after a person falls asleep. People have between three and five REM phases a night. They are not awake, but the brain is awake and active. People dream during REM sleep, but the body cannot move. That stops people from "acting" their dreams.

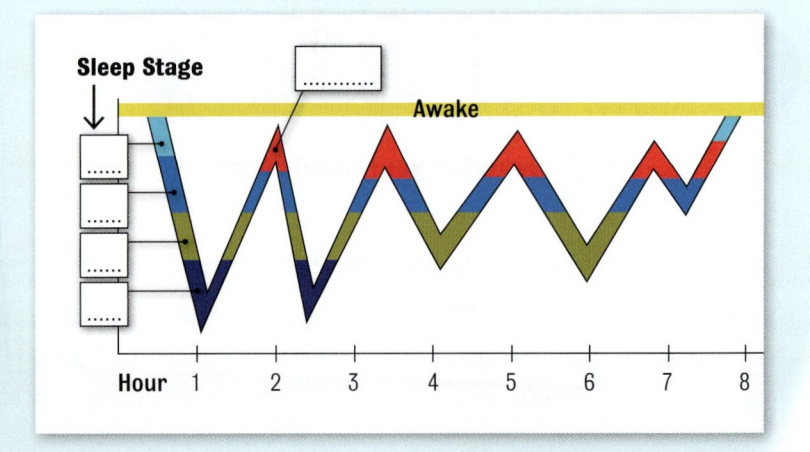

**Stage four**
Breathing is rhythmic. There is some muscle activity. It is difficult to wake up from this sleep.

## FACT FILE

- You should sleep for about 8 to 10 hours each night.
- Human babies sleep for about 16 hours a day.
- Older people sleep for just 5 to 6 hours a night.
- Some animals sleep during the day. They are active during the night.
- Other animals hibernate— they "sleep" for 3 to 4 months during the winter.

**2** Answer the questions.

1. How many non-REM stages of sleep are there?
2. When is the heartbeat at its slowest?
3. How many sleep cycles do people have each night?
4. What part of the body moves when a person dreams?

48 UNIT 3

## How animals sleep

Most animals sleep in cycles of non-REM and REM sleep. But not all animals sleep the same number of hours. What is important for animals is how safe they are when they are asleep. If an animal is in danger (for example, if other animals hunt it for food) then it will sleep fewer hours.

**3** Read the texts below and match them to the correct photo. Write the correct letter for each photo.

A  Leopards often sleep in trees. There, they are safe from lions.

B  Bats sleep for almost 20 hours a day. Almost four hours is REM sleep.

C  Giraffes sleep for about 4.5 hours a day. They have about 30 minutes of REM sleep.

D  Lions sleep for about 13.5 hours a day. They only get up to drink. They hunt during the night.

E  Dolphins sleep for 10 hours a day, but only half of their brain is asleep. About 15 minutes is REM sleep.

### Mini-project

**4** Keep a sleep diary for a week. Make a note of

- what time you go to bed
- what time you wake up
- if you dream
- how many times you wake up during the night
- if you nap during the day
- how many hours you sleep each day in total

**5** After a week, compare your sleep diaries in class.

**MORE!** Now you can watch Episode 3 of *The Story of the Stones.*

# UNIT 4 Who's that boy?

### In this unit

**You learn**
- have/has
- the articles *a/an*
- parts of the body
- countries and nationalities

**and then you can**
- talk about nationality
- describe people
- talk about possessions

### 1 Listen and read.

**Kate** I have some news.
**Nicole** Oh? What?
**Kate** There's a new guy in my brother's class!
**Nicole** Oh really?
**Kate** Yeah, he's Brazilian, I think. Or Bolivian, perhaps—I'm not sure. His name's Davi.
**Nicole** Davi? Well, he's probably Brazilian. It's a Brazilian name. Is he cute?
**Kate** Yeah—he's tall, and he has dark hair and brown eyes. And he's 14.
**Nicole** Nice! Does he have an accent?

**Kate** Yes, he does. It's great. I think foreign accents are really cool!
**Nicole** Me too! Oh look! Is that him?
**Kate** Yes, it is—oh no, he's with Isabella!
**Nicole** Oh well, Kate. Look, the bus is here.
**Kate** Are they together?
**Nicole** I don't know, but you have a bus pass. Get on first and try to sit next to him!

**2** Correct the wrong information in each sentence.

1. There's a new girl in Kate's brother's class.   ........guy........
2. The boy's name is Daniel.   ....................
3. He has green eyes.   ....................
4. He's short.   ....................
5. Davi is 15.   ....................
6. Kate is happy that Davi's with Isabella.   ....................

## Vocabulary  Countries and nationalities

**3** Write the name of the country and the nationality in the correct place.

Chile/Chilean
Peru/Peruvian
Japan/Japanese
~~Colombia/Colombian~~
Australia/Australian
Panama/Panamanian
Philippines/Filipino
China/Chinese

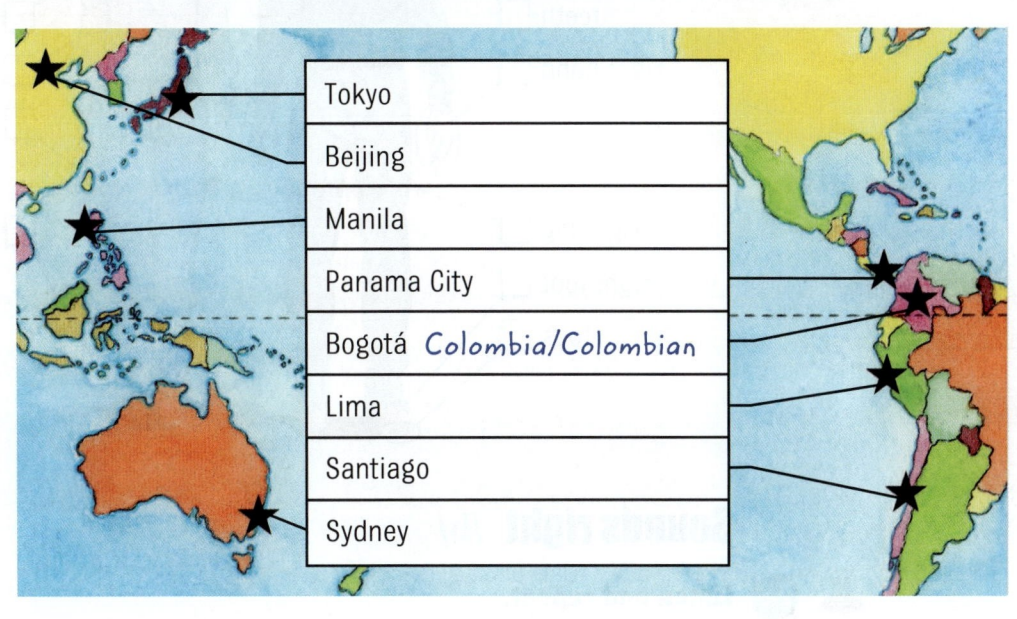

| |
|---|
| Tokyo |
| Beijing |
| Manila |
| Panama City |
| Bogotá   Colombia/Colombian |
| Lima |
| Santiago |
| Sydney |

**4** Listen and check.

**5** Listen and repeat.

| ① | ② | ③ | ④ | ⑤ | ⑥ | ⑦ | ⑧ |
|---|---|---|---|---|---|---|---|
| **Brazil** | **China** | **Britain** | **The U.S.** | **Japan** | **Mexico** | **Ecuador** | **Haiti** |
| Brazilian | Chinese | British | American | Japanese | Mexican | Ecuadorian | Haitian |

## Get talking  Talking about nationality

**6** Ask and answer with a partner.

A  Where's she from?
B  She's from Brazil.

A  Oh, she's Brazilian.
B  That's right.

UNIT 4  51

# Language Focus

## Vocabulary  Parts of the body

**38  1** Listen and write the numbers next to the words.

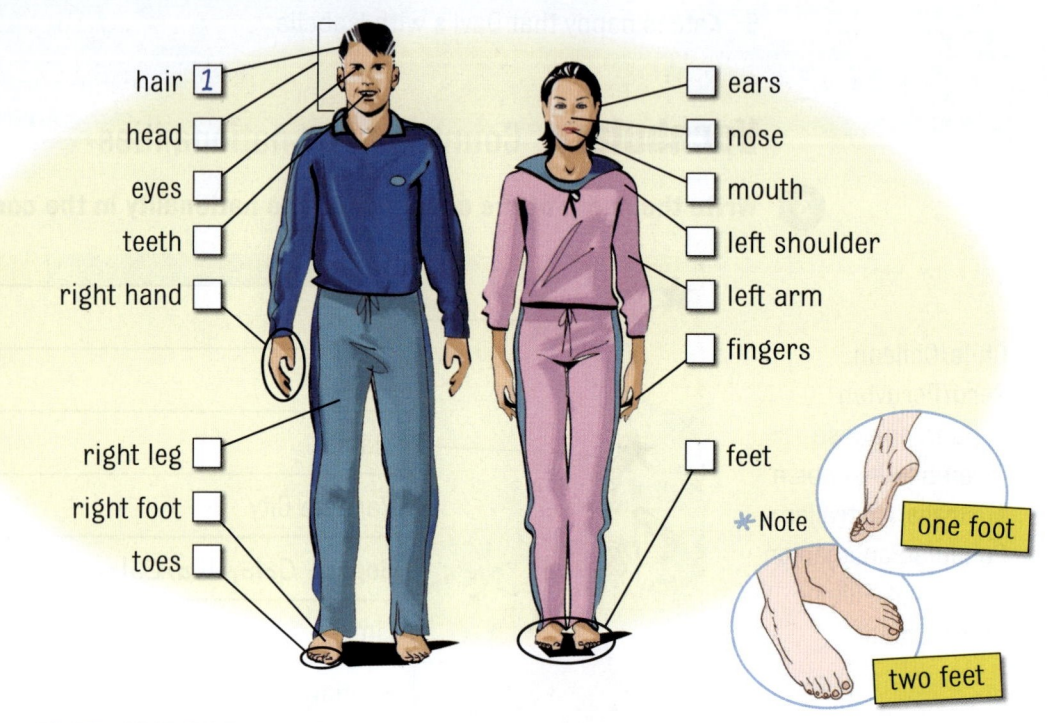

hair [1]
head
eyes
teeth
right hand
right leg
right foot
toes

ears
nose
mouth
left shoulder
left arm
fingers
feet

*Note

one foot

two feet

## Sounds right  /h/

**39  2a** Listen and repeat.

1  hand    2  happy    3  head    4  hungry    5  hair    6  her

**40  2b**  1  Put your hands on your head.
2  Is he happy or hungry?

## Get talking  Describing people

**3** Work with a partner. Describe one of the pictures below and ask your partner which one it is.

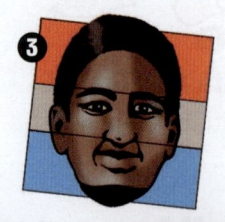

❶ ❷ ❸ ❹ ❺ ❻

**A** He has short hair, blue eyes, and a big nose.

**B** It's number two.

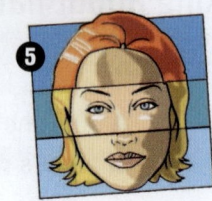

**A** That's right.

52  UNIT 4

# Grammar

## have/has

**1** Look at the examples from the dialogue on page 50. Complete the table.

He **has** dark hair.   **Does** he **have** an accent? Yes, he **does**.
You **have** a bus pass.

| Affirmative | | |
|---|---|---|
| I/you/we/they | **have** | long hair. |
| He/she/it | 1 ............ | brown eyes. |

| Negative | | |
|---|---|---|
| I/you/we/they | **don't have** | long hair. |
| He/she/it | 2 ............ | a bus pass. |

| Questions | | | Short answers | |
|---|---|---|---|---|
| | | | Affirmative | Negative |
| **Do** I/you/we/they | 4 ............ | an accent? | Yes, I/you/we/they **do**. | No, I/you/we/they **don't**. |
| 3 ............ he/she/it | | | Yes, he/she/it 5 ............ | No, he/she/it **doesn't**. |

**2** Complete with *have* or *has*.

1 They _have_ three cats.
2 He ............ a small nose.
3 She ............ green eyes.
4 I ............ long hair.
5 We ............ a big dog.
6 You ............ a cool accent.

**3** Complete with the correct form of *have*.

1 My friend _has_ three dogs.
2 I ............ some news.
3 You ............ nice hair.
4 My dog ............ long ears.
5 They ............ good ice cream in that place.
6 She ............ a new DVD player.
7 He ............ a French accent.
8 My brother and I ............ green eyes.

**4** Write sentences using the negative form.

1 He has a dog. _He doesn't have a dog._
2 I have long hair.
   ............................................
3 My mom has a new car.
   ............................................
4 We have a big house.
   ............................................
5 You have an accent.
   ............................................
6 The cat has blue eyes.
   ............................................

**5** Reorder the words to ask questions.

1 cat / do / a / have / you
   _Do you have a cat_ ?
2 computer / does / she / have / a
   ............................................ ?
3 eyes / he / brown / does / have
   ............................................ ?
4 they / black / do / hair / have
   ............................................ ?
5 we / do / a / have / teacher / new
   ............................................ ?

## 6 Write short answers.

1. Does he have a cat?
   *Yes, he does.* It's black and white.
2. Does she have black hair?
   ........................... It's brown.
3. Do they have an accent?
   ..........................., and it's very nice!
4. Do you have a new teacher?
   ..........................., she's great!
5. Do we have any ice cream?
   ..........................., but we do have yogurt.

## Get talking  Talking about possessions

### 7 Listen and complete.

41

1. **A** Do you have ¹........................... in your room?
   **B** Yes, I do.
   **A** What ²........................... are they?
   **B** They're ³........................... .

2. **A** Do you have a ¹...........................?
   **B** Yes, I do.
   **A** How ²........................... is she?
   **B** She's ³........................... She has ⁴........................... eyes and long hair.
   **A** What's her ⁵...........................?
   **B** Joanna.

3. **A** Do you have a ¹...........................?
   **B** Yes, we do.
   **A** What's its ²...........................?
   **B** Blackie.
   **A** What ³........................... is it?
   **B** ⁴..........................., of course.
   **A** How ⁵........................... is it?
   **B** Um, ⁶..........................., I think.

## 8 Work with a partner. Ask and answer questions about people, animals, and things.

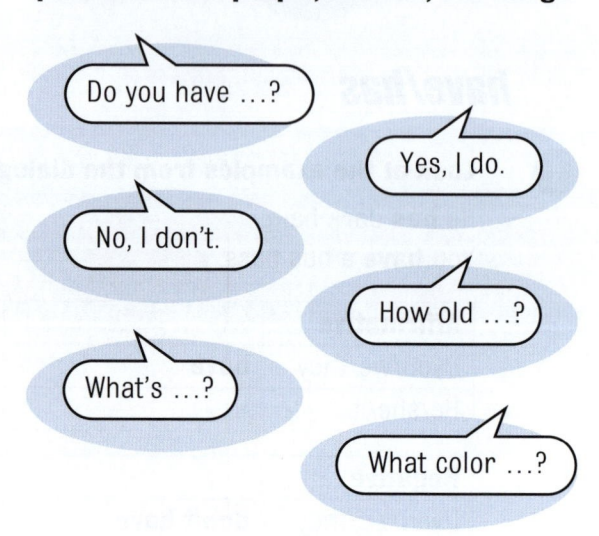

- Do you have …?
- Yes, I do.
- No, I don't.
- How old …?
- What's …?
- What color …?

## The indefinite article

### 9 Look at the examples and complete the rule.

| | | | |
|---|---|---|---|
| a | book | an | apple |
| a | car | an | eye |
| a | house | an | ice cream |
| a | pen | an | orange |
| a | room | an | umbrella |

* Before a noun that starts with a consonant use ¹............
* Before a noun that starts with a vowel use ²............

### 10 Complete with *a* or *an*.

1. I have ...*a*... banana and an apple.
2. Look! It's ............ black cat!
3. There's ............ armchair in my bedroom.
4. There's ............ great ice cream place in town.

54 UNIT 4

# Skills

## Listening

**42**

**1** Listen and write the correct name in the box.

Linda
Alice
Barbara
Tom
Frank
Chris

## Reading

**2** Read the texts and match them to the correct picture.

*Ellen* is 14 years old. She's Chinese. She's from Hong Kong. She has long, black hair. Her eyes are brown.

*Maria* is 14 years old. She's Mexican. She's from Guadalajara. She has long, dark hair and brown eyes.

*Sylvie* is 13 years old. She's American. She's from Chicago. She has short, brown hair and blue eyes.

UNIT 4  55

## Speaking

**3** Look at the photos of teenagers of various nationalities (Italian, English, German, French, Spanish, and Portuguese). Discuss the nationality of each one and try to guess where they are from.

**A** I think the girl in photo 5 is from Spain.

**B** I think so, too.

**A** I think the boy in photo 2 is from Germany.

**B** I don't think so. I think he's from Portugal.

## Writing for your Portfolio

**4** Read the text and describe yourself or a friend.

My pen pal's name is Hiroto. He's 13. He's Japanese. He's from Kyoto. He has black hair and brown eyes. He has a computer with lots of video games.

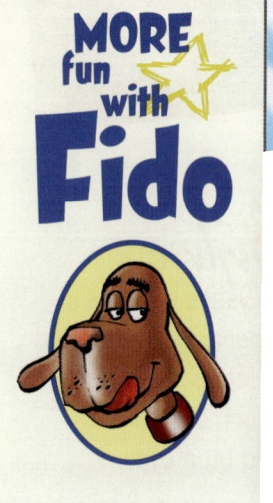

### MORE fun with Fido

Come here!

Now I have got you!

# Check your progress  Units 3 and 4

**1** In which rooms can you find these things?

1. oven, fridge ........................
2. wardrobe, bed ........................
3. armchair, TV ........................
4. sink, bathtub ........................
5. car, bicycle ........................

☐ 5

**2** Circle the correct answer.

1. There *is / are* two English girls in my school.
2. *Is / Are* there a good movie on tonight?
3. There *isn't / aren't* a zoo in my town.
4. There *is / are* a lot of chairs in the classroom.
5. *Is / Are* there blue curtains in your room?
6. There *isn't / aren't* a lot of people in the theater.

☐ 6

**3** Put a check mark next to the correct sentences and correct the wrong ones.

1. There are three black dogs in the park. ☐
2. Philadelphia is a city beautiful. ☐
3. There is two good actors in the movie. ☐
4. Are there two new CDs in your bag? ☐
5. There is six books under my desk. ☐

☐ 5

**4** Write *P* if the '*s* is possessive or *A* if it is an abbreviation of *is*.

1. John's dogs are very friendly. ........
2. Where's your school? ........
3. Alison's not very happy today. ........
4. My mother's in her bedroom. ........
5. Susie's backpack is green and blue. ........
6. My cat's under the car. ........

☐ 6

**5** Complete with the correct form of *have*.

1. My brother ........................ a new skateboard.
2. I ........................ a lot of homework.
3. ................ you ................ a big house?
4. She ........................ long, brown hair.
5. They ........................ two sisters.
6. My teacher ........................ a new motorcycle.

☐ 6

**6** Complete the table.

| Country | Nationality |
|---|---|
| 1 ............ | Brazilian |
| Colombia | 4 ............ |
| 2 ............ | Bolivian |
| Panama | 5 ............ |
| 3 ............ | Argentinian |
| Chile | 6 ............ |

☐ 6

**7** Write the names for parts of the body.

1. ysee ........................
2. gnfire ........................
3. thoum ........................
4. hetet ........................
5. drehsluo ........................
6. sote ........................

☐ 6

**8** Answer the questions.

1. Do you have a bicycle?
   ........................
2. What color hair do you have?
   ........................
3. Does your teacher have a Brazilian accent?
   ........................
4. Do your parents have a Japanese car?
   ........................

☐ 10

TOTAL ☐ 50

**My progress so far is ...**

☺ great! ☐
😐 good. ☐
☹ poor. ☐

UNIT 4  57

# School in the U.S.

**1** Read the information about Sarah and complete the sentences with colors.

Hi, I'm Sarah. I'm 14 years old. I'm a freshman in high school. I go to a large school in the Midwest. I play the saxophone in our school marching band. I have to wear a uniform.

The shirt is ..................... .
The neck strap is ..................... .
The hat is ..................... .

### FACT FILE

**The American School System**
**Age** 5 to 18 years old
**Elementary School** 5 to 11 years old
**Junior High or Middle School** 11 to 14 years old (varies)
**High School** 14 to 18 years old (varies)

**2** Look at the symbols and say which subject they are.

1 is music.

**3** Listen and complete Sarah's class schedule.

| Time | MONDAY | TUESDAY | WEDNESDAY | THURSDAY | FRIDAY |
|---|---|---|---|---|---|
| 8:30 | ATTENDANCE | | | | |
| 8:45 | 1............ | French | 3............ | Earth Science | Biology |
| 9:25 | 2............ | English | 4............ | Earth Science | Biology |
| 10:00 | BREAK | | | | |
| 10:30 | German | History | Earth Science | Math | English |
| 11:15 | History | Math | English | English | |
| 12:00 | LUNCHTIME | | | | |
| 12:45 | English | P.E. | Geography | 5............ | History |
| 1:30 | Math | P.E. | Music | 6............ | Art |
| 2:15 | Computer Science | P.E. | Music | 7............ | 8............ |
| 3:00 | END OF SCHOOL DAY | | | | |

**4** **Over 2 U!** Write your schedule in English in your notebook.

**MORE!** Now you can watch Episode 4 of *The Story of the Stones*.

58 UNIT 4

# The wide-mouthed frog

"Hi. I'm a wide-mouthed frog!"

| | |
|---|---|
| **Frog** | Hi. How are you? |
| **Gorilla** | I'm fine, thanks. What's your name? |
| **Frog** | I'm Freddy. I'm a wide-mouthed frog, and my favorite food is flies. What's your name? |
| **Gorilla** | I'm Gordon. I'm a gorilla. My favorite food is bananas. |
| **Frog** | Well, nice to meet you! Bye, gorilla! |
| **Gorilla** | Bye, frog! |

..................................................................

| | |
|---|---|
| **Frog** | Hi. How are you? |
| **Bear** | I'm fine, thanks. What's your name? |
| **Frog** | I'm Freddy. I'm a wide-mouthed frog. My favorite food is flies. What's your name? |
| **Bear** | I'm Betty. I'm a bear. My favorite food is honey. |
| **Frog** | Well, nice to meet you! Bye, bear! |
| **Bear** | Bye, frog! |

..................................................................

| | |
|---|---|
| **Frog** | Hi. How are you? |
| **Crocodile** | I'm fine, thanks. What's your name? |
| **Frog** | I'm Freddy. I'm a wide-mouthed frog. My favorite food is flies. What's your name? |
| **Crocodile** | I'm Carl. I'm a crocodile. My favorite food is … wide-mouthed frogs! |
| **Frog** | Oh no, oh no, oh no! Bye! |

!!!

For **MORE!** Go to www.more-online.com/american and take a quiz about this text.

UNIT 4

# UNIT 5 What's for lunch?

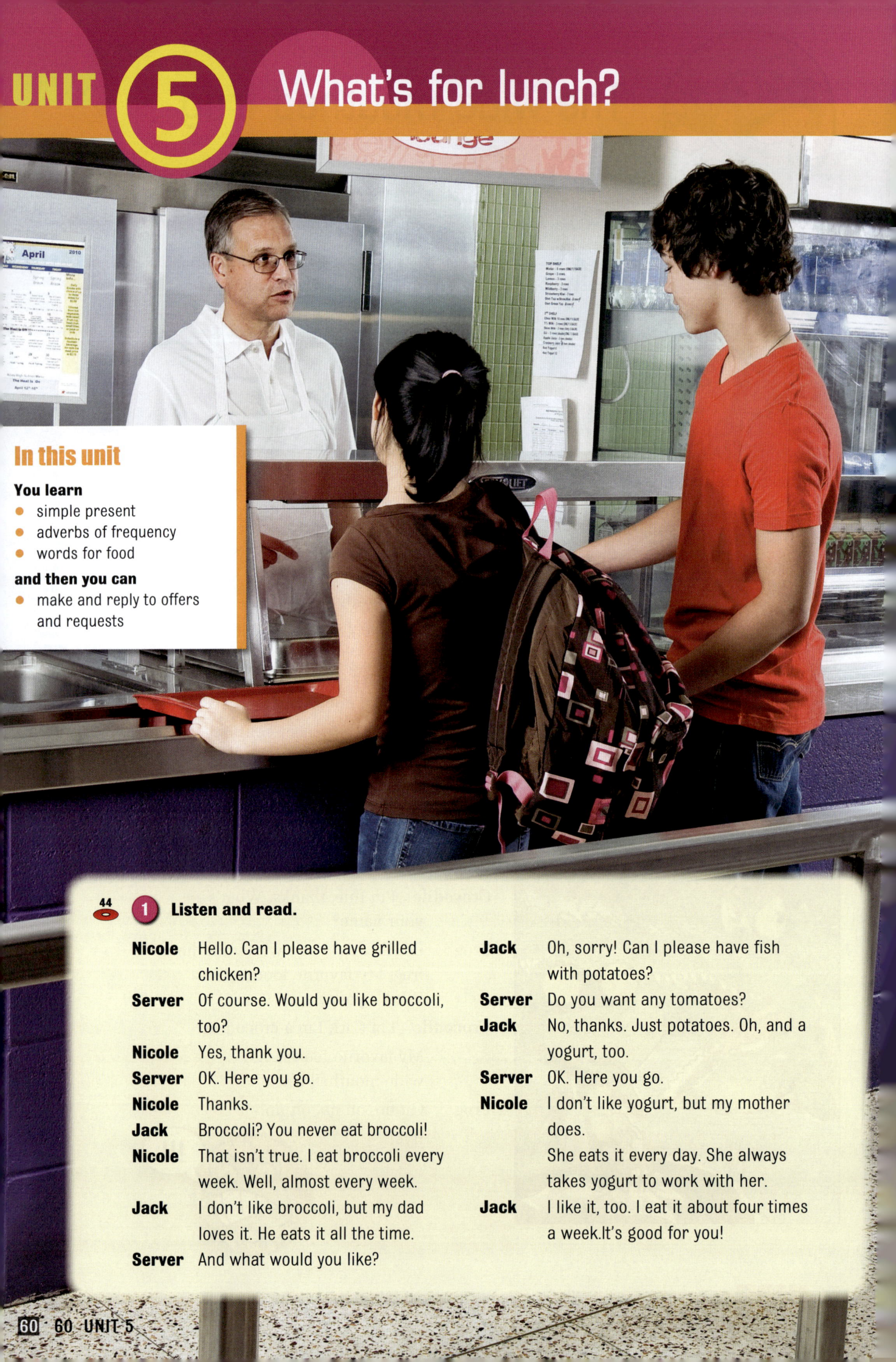

### In this unit

**You learn**
- simple present
- adverbs of frequency
- words for food

**and then you can**
- make and reply to offers and requests

**1  Listen and read.**

| | |
|---|---|
| **Nicole** | Hello. Can I please have grilled chicken? |
| **Server** | Of course. Would you like broccoli, too? |
| **Nicole** | Yes, thank you. |
| **Server** | OK. Here you go. |
| **Nicole** | Thanks. |
| **Jack** | Broccoli? You never eat broccoli! |
| **Nicole** | That isn't true. I eat broccoli every week. Well, almost every week. |
| **Jack** | I don't like broccoli, but my dad loves it. He eats it all the time. |
| **Server** | And what would you like? |
| **Jack** | Oh, sorry! Can I please have fish with potatoes? |
| **Server** | Do you want any tomatoes? |
| **Jack** | No, thanks. Just potatoes. Oh, and a yogurt, too. |
| **Server** | OK. Here you go. |
| **Nicole** | I don't like yogurt, but my mother does. She eats it every day. She always takes yogurt to work with her. |
| **Jack** | I like it, too. I eat it about four times a week. It's good for you! |

### 2 Circle T (True) or F (False) for the sentences below.

1 Nicole wants grilled chicken.  T / F
2 Nicole never eats broccoli.  T / F
3 Jack likes broccoli.  T / F
4 Jack's father likes broccoli.  T / F
5 Jack wants fish with tomatoes.  T / F
6 Nicole doesn't like yogurt.  T / F

### 3 Read the dialogue on page 60 again, and then fill in the blanks.

**Nicole**  Hello. May I please have grilled chicken?
**Server**  Of course ¹............................................ broccoli, too?
**Nicole**  Yes, ²............................................ .
**Server**  OK. ³............................................ .

**Server**  ⁴............................................ tomatoes?
**Jack**  No, ⁵............................................ .

### 4 Listen and circle the correct word or expression.

1  **A**  banana / apple
   **B**  Yes, please. / No, thanks.

2  **A**  orange / apple
   **B**  Yes, please. / No, thanks.

3  **A**  sandwich / hamburger
   **B**  Yes, please. / No, thanks.

4  **A**  ice cream / yogurt
   **B**  Yes, please. / No, thanks.

## Get talking  Making and replying to polite offers

### 5 Work with a partner. Ask and answer questions using the pictures below.

1. Would you like a sandwich?
   Yes, please. / No, thanks.

2. Would you like ........................?
   Yes, please. / No, thanks.

3. Would you like ........................?
   Yes, please. / No, thanks.

4. Would you like ........................?
   Yes, please. / No, thanks.

5. Would you like ........................?
   Yes, please. / No, thanks.

6. Would you like ........................?
   Yes, please. / No, thanks.

# Language Focus

## Vocabulary  Food

**1** 🎧 46  Listen and write the numbers.

| ☐ onions | ☐ tea | ☐ egg | ☐ rice | ☐ bread | ☐ fish |
| ☐ cherries | ☐ chicken | ☐ oranges | ☐ milk | ☐ potatoes | ☐ coffee |
| ☐ sausages | ☐ grapes | ☐ spinach | ☐ apples | ☐ carrots | ☐ orange juice |

**2**  Write the words from Exercise 1 under the correct category.

| Drinks | Vegetables | Fruit | Meat | Others |
| ............ | ............ | ............ | ............ | ............ |

## Sounds right  Question intonation

**3** 🎧 47  Listen and repeat.

1  May I have fish?
2  Would you like a sandwich?
3  Can I have an apple?
4  Would you like a banana?

## Get talking  Polite requests

**4**  Work in pairs. Read the dialogue. Use the pictures to make different dialogues.

**Boy**     Can I please have chicken and rice?
**Server**  Yes, of course. Here you go.

❶ ❷ ❸
❹ ❺ ❻

62  UNIT 5

# Grammar

## Simple present Affirmative

**1** Use the examples from the dialogue on page 60 to complete the table.

I eat broccoli every week.
My dad loves it.
She eats it every day.

| I/you/we/they | love | yogurt. |
|---|---|---|
| He/she/it | 1 .............. | |

**2** Put the words in the correct order and make sentences.

1 watch / television / I / on Sunday
..................................................
2 homework / you / do / at home
..................................................
3 likes / my / spaghetti / mother
..................................................
4 fish / eat / on Friday / we
..................................................
5 Shakira / to / he / listens
..................................................
6 on Monday / hate / school / they
..................................................

## Spelling Third person singular

**Notice the spellings.**

| Rela**x** | My dad always relax**es** after breakfast on Saturday. |
| Ki**ss** | She kiss**es** her mom goodbye. |
| Wa**sh** | He wash**es** his bike on Saturday. |
| Do | Mary do**es** the laundry. |
| Carr**y** | Steve carr**ies** the bags for his mom. |
| Watch | Jenny watch**es** DVDs every day. |

**3** Complete the sentences with the correct form of the verb.

1 My brother always .............. (miss) the bus!
2 She .............. (relax) on the weekend.
3 She .............. (wash) her dog on Saturday.
4 Mike .............. (watch) football on Sundays.
5 My sister .............. (clean) her room all the time.
6 Jenny .............. (do) her homework in the evening.

**4** Complete the sentences with the correct form of the verb.

1 I ....*love*.... (love) chicken sandwiches.
2 Steve .............. (like) yogurt.
3 My brother and I .............. (hate) baseball.
4 Her mother .............. (take) her to school every day.
5 My father .............. (teach) French at our school.
6 Sarah .............. (go) to the movies on Saturday.
7 You .............. (relax) on the weekend.
8 They .............. (eat) chicken on Sunday.

**5** Complete the sentences using the words below.

| takes | eat | go | watches |
| goes | watch | take | eats |

1 I .............. DVDs on my computer.
2 We .............. to school on Monday morning.
3 Kevin .............. an apple after lunch.
4 Jack .............. a bus to the football stadium.
5 I .............. my brother to school.
6 My sister .............. TV every day.
7 They .............. a lot of fish.
8 Hal .............. to the mall every Saturday morning.

UNIT 5

## Adverbs of frequency

**6** Read the examples and complete the rule.

I **often** play soccer.
I am **never** late.

* Frequency adverbs usually go ¹........................ the main verb.
* But they go ²........................ the verb *be*.

| 100% | I always | |
| --- | --- | --- |
| ↑ | I usually | eat popcorn |
| | I often | at the |
| ↓ | I sometimes | movies. |
| 0% | I never | |

**7** Translate the words into your own language.

| 100% | always | ........................ |
| --- | --- | --- |
| | usually | ........................ |
| | often | ........................ |
| | sometimes | ........................ |
| 0% | never | ........................ |

**8** Reorder the words and write sentences.

1 never / is / my father / late
   *My father is never late.*

2 is / Nicole / usually / hungry
   ........................................................

3 often / am / nervous / I
   ........................................................

4 goes / she / to the movies / often
   ........................................................

5 watches / sometimes / Jo / football on TV
   ........................................................

6 usually / eat / breakfast / I / at home
   ........................................................

**9** Put the adverb in the correct place.

1 I watch TV on Sunday. (always)
2 My brother does his homework. (never)
3 James and Sally are hungry. (usually)
4 Our teacher is mad at us. (always)
5 Nicole and Kate go to the movies together. (sometimes)
6 You are late. (often)

Tom never washes his dog!

**10** Listen and complete the sentences.

48

| sometimes | drink | always |
| --- | --- | --- |
| eat | often | have | never |

1 I ........................ coffee at breakfast.
2 I ........................ soup for lunch.
3 I ........................ milk.
4 I ........................ eggs for breakfast.
5 We ........................ fish on Friday.
6 I ........................ rice and fish.

**11** Talk about your favorite food.

I love chicken soup.
I never eat onions.

I hate bananas.
I often eat hamburgers.

UNIT 5

# Skills

**Get talking** Talking about what we eat

**1** Read and check the correct answer.

## What do you eat?

**1** I eat hamburgers or hot dogs
- ☐ every day.
- ☐ three times a week.
- ☐ once a week.
- ☐ once a month.
- ☐ I never eat hamburgers or hot dogs.

**2** I eat vegetables
- ☐ every day.
- ☐ three times a week.
- ☐ once a week.
- ☐ once a month.
- ☐ I never eat vegetables.

**3** I eat fruit
- ☐ every day.
- ☐ three times a week.
- ☐ once a week.
- ☐ once a month.
- ☐ I never eat fruit.

**4** I eat chocolate, ice cream, or candy
- ☐ every day.
- ☐ three times a week.
- ☐ once a week.
- ☐ once a month.
- ☐ I never eat sweets.

**2** Work in groups of six to eight and talk about what you eat. Then share with the class.

> Two people in our group eat hamburgers or hot dogs three times a week.

UNIT 5

## Reading

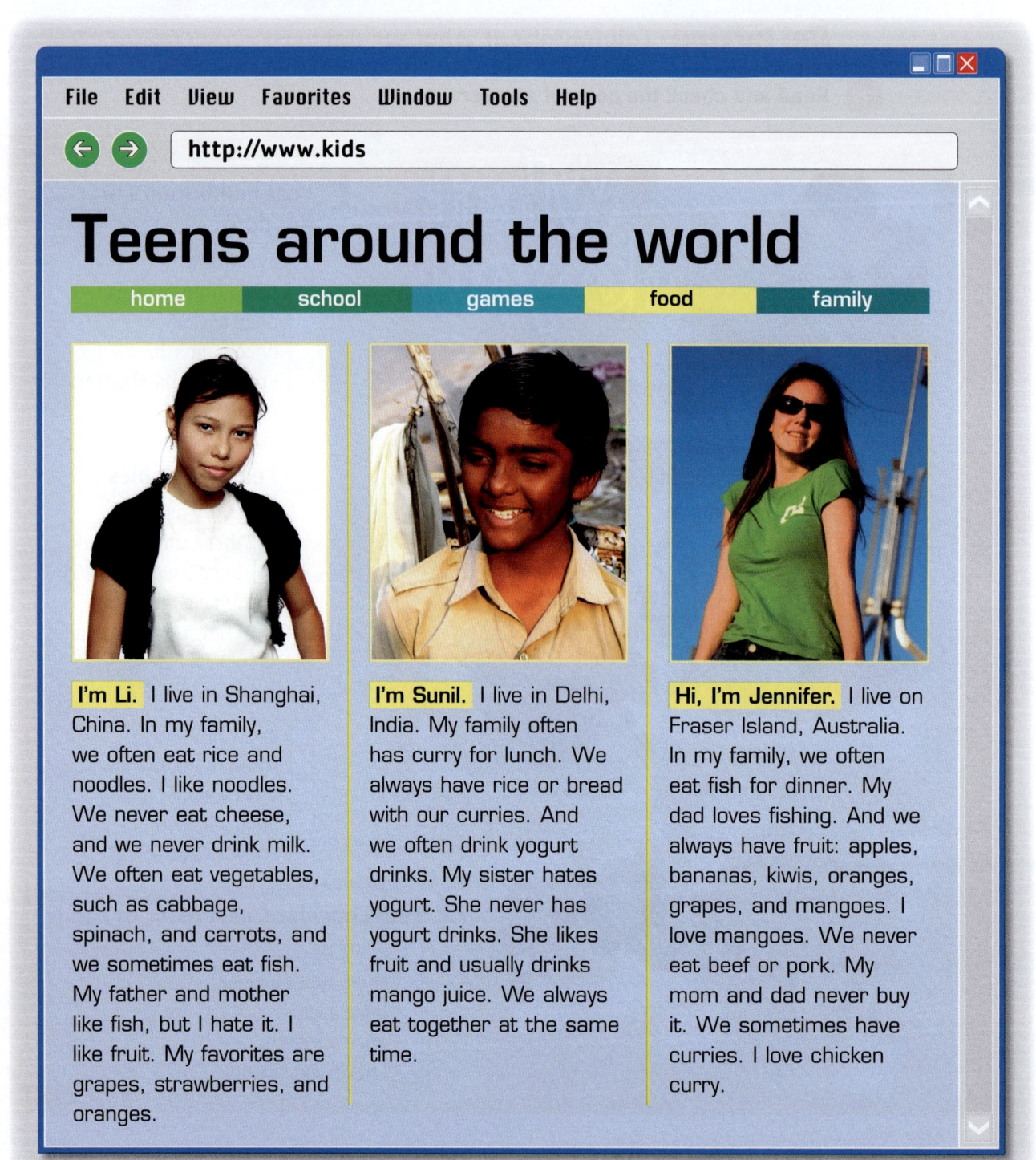

**1** Read the texts.

# Teens around the world

home | school | games | food | family

**I'm Li.** I live in Shanghai, China. In my family, we often eat rice and noodles. I like noodles. We never eat cheese, and we never drink milk. We often eat vegetables, such as cabbage, spinach, and carrots, and we sometimes eat fish. My father and mother like fish, but I hate it. I like fruit. My favorites are grapes, strawberries, and oranges.

**I'm Sunil.** I live in Delhi, India. My family often has curry for lunch. We always have rice or bread with our curries. And we often drink yogurt drinks. My sister hates yogurt. She never has yogurt drinks. She likes fruit and usually drinks mango juice. We always eat together at the same time.

**Hi, I'm Jennifer.** I live on Fraser Island, Australia. In my family, we often eat fish for dinner. My dad loves fishing. And we always have fruit: apples, bananas, kiwis, oranges, grapes, and mangoes. I love mangoes. We never eat beef or pork. My mom and dad never buy it. We sometimes have curries. I love chicken curry.

**2** Circle T (True) or F (False) for the sentences below.

1. Li's family often eats rice and noodles.   T / F
2. Sunil's sister hates yogurt drinks.   T / F
3. Jennifer's family sometimes eats fish.   T / F
4. Li's family sometimes eats vegetables.   T / F
5. Sunil's family often has rice or bread with curry.   T / F
6. Jennifer doesn't like mangoes.   T / F

## Listening

**3** Complete the dialogue using the words on the left.

new
don't have
thanks
May I have a
There is no
fast food

| | |
|---|---|
| **Teacher** | ¹.............................. hamburger, please? |
| **Server** | Sorry, no hamburgers. |
| **Teacher** | OK. May I have a hot dog, then? |
| **Server** | Sorry, we ².............................. any hot dogs. |
| **Jack** | *(to Nicole)* Is he ³..............................? |
| **Nicole** | Yes, he is. |
| **Jack** | ⁴.............................. junk food here. |
| **Nicole** | But there's a ⁵.............................. place around the corner. |
| **Teacher** | I won't have anything, but ⁶.............................. anyway. |
| **Jack** | Can I come with you? |

**4** Listen and check.

# Writing for your Portfolio

**5** Read the text and describe your eating habits.

I always have juice for breakfast. I sometimes eat scrambled eggs. My younger brother never eats eggs. He likes to eat toast. For lunch, we often have salad. We sometimes have pizza. On Sunday, we sometimes go to a restaurant and have my favorite food—pizza!

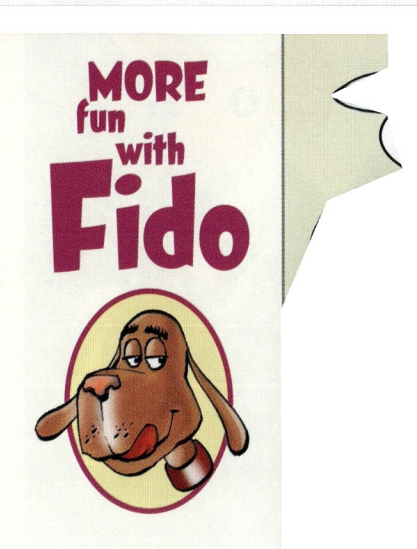

**MORE fun with Fido**

# Food from around the world

The foods people eat in different countries depend on many different factors.

**1  a  Look at the list below. What do you think are important factors?**

| climate | money | national flag | culture |
|---------|-------|---------------|---------|
| sports | religion | holidays | |

**Key words**
export
produce
population
shrimp
olive oil
wheat
import
necessity
climate
commodity

**b  Now read the text and check your answers.**

People eat different foods in different countries. Why? There are many reasons. The climate can play a role. More fruits and vegetables are often grown in hot, sunny places. People's religion and culture are also important. People of some religions do not eat certain foods. People also travel more today so they try food from countries. Of course, how much money you have also counts. If you don't have much money, you can't always buy the best food.

**2  a  What food can you see in the photos?**

**b  From what country do you think this food comes? Compare your ideas with a partner.**

**3  Look at the map. Write the numbers of the countries next to the names. Listen and check.**

☐ Brazil   ☐ Egypt   ☐ The U.S.
☐ China    ☐ Ecuador ☐ Italy

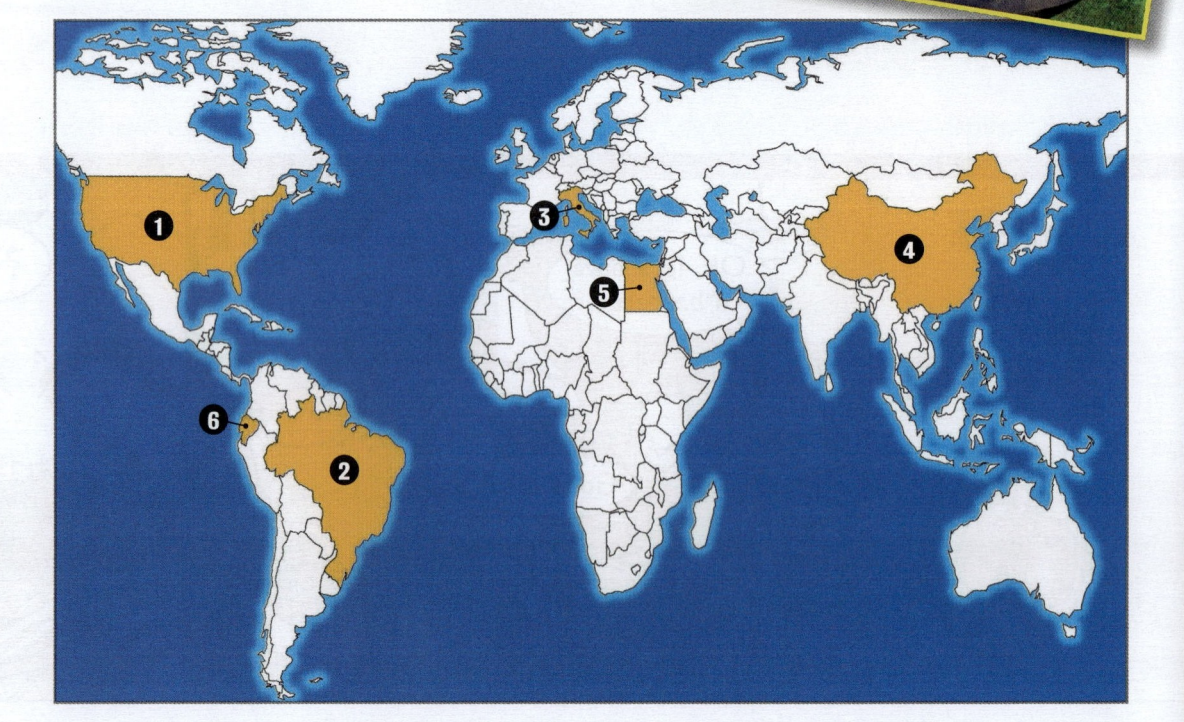

68  UNIT 5

**4** Listen to the dialogue and draw the symbols on the map.

| chicken | rice | pasta | oranges | bananas | potatoes |

## International trade

Food is a necessity. We all need to eat, but food is also an important commodity for many countries. Countries can sell (export) their food to other countries or buy (import) food from other countries.

**5** Read the sentences. Which of the countries in Exercise 3 are they about?

1 The capital city is Quito. People speak Spanish here. This country exports a lot of bananas and shrimp.
........................

2 The capital city is Brasilia. People speak Portuguese here. This country produces and exports a lot of coffee, sugar, and soybeans.
........................

3 The capital city is Rome. This country produces a lot of olive oil and pasta.
........................

4 The capital city is Cairo. People speak Arabic here. This country produces fresh fruit and vegetables.
........................

5 The capital city is Washington, D.C. This country produces a lot of wheat and rice. It is famous for having foods from many cultures.
........................

6 The capital city is Beijing. This country has the biggest population in the world. People eat a lot of fish and rice.
........................

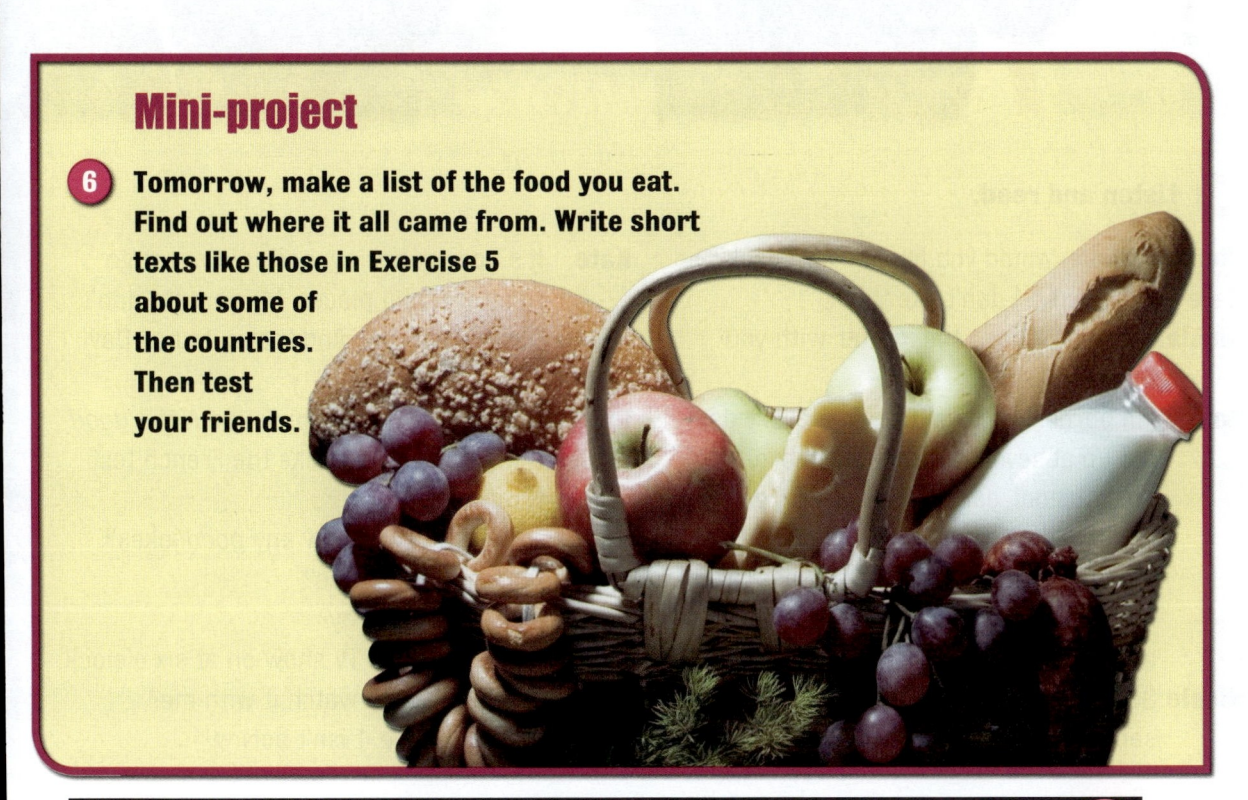

## Mini-project

**6** Tomorrow, make a list of the food you eat. Find out where it all came from. Write short texts like those in Exercise 5 about some of the countries. Then test your friends.

**MORE!** Now you can watch Episode 5 of *The Story of the Stones*.

# UNIT 6 Time for a change

**In this unit**

You learn
- simple present (negatives, questions, and short answers)
- object pronouns
- words for daily activities

and then you can
- ask and tell the time
- talk about routines

## 1  Listen and read.

**Nicole** Hi, Kate. Would you like a fruit snack?
**Kate** No, thanks. I don't like them.
**Nicole** Why not? What's the matter with you today?
**Kate** I'm bored. My life's the same every day. I get up at seven o'clock, I have breakfast, go to school, eat a boring lunch, go home, do my homework, and then I have dinner, play on the computer, and go to bed at nine thirty. The next day, I get up and do it again!
**Nicole** So what? What's the problem? It's the same for me.
**Kate** It's boring, boring, boring! I never go to interesting places. My parents don't understand me. And that cute boy Davi doesn't like me!
**Nicole** Don't worry, Kate! Think about the *good* things in your life, like the French test tomorrow.
**Kate** Ha, ha! Do you know any *good* jokes? Oh, what's the time?
**Nicole** It's ten to six. Why?
**Kate** There's a good TV show on at six o'clock. Do you want to watch it with me?
**Nicole** OK. But I hope it isn't boring!

**2** **Circle the correct answer.**

1 Kate is *bored* / *happy* .
2 Kate gets up at *6:00* / *7:00* .
3 She goes to bed at *9:15* / *9:30*.
4 Kate's parents *understand* / *don't understand* her.
5 There's a French *class* / *test* at school tomorrow.

## Get talking  Asking and telling the time

**3** **Listen and read.**

① It's three o'clock. 
② It's five past three. 
③ It's ten past three. 
④ It's a quarter past three. 
⑤ It's twenty past three. 
⑥ It's twenty-five past three. 
⑦ It's three thirty. 
⑧ It's twenty-five to four. 
⑨ It's twenty to four. 
⑩ It's a quarter to four. 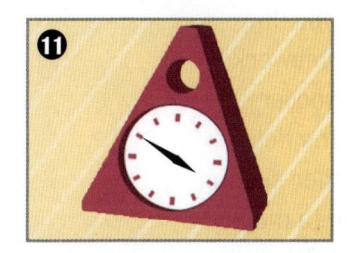
⑪ It's ten to four. 
⑫ It's five to four.

**4** **Work with a partner. Cover a clock from Exercise 3 and ask and answer about the time.**

What's the time?   It's twenty to four.

UNIT 6

# Language Focus

## Vocabulary  Daily activities

**1** Listen and write the phrases under the correct pictures.

watch TV
~~go shopping~~
do homework
listen to music
walk the dog
go roller-skating
hang out with friends
play computer games
read a book
play the piano
surf the Net
play soccer

1. go shopping
2. ...................
3. ...................
4. ...................
5. ...................
6. ...................
7. ...................
8. ...................
9. ...................
10. ...................
11. ...................
12. ...................

## Get talking  Talking about routines

**2** Listen and put a check next to the activities that Ben and Lisa do.

**LISA**
- [ ] walk the dog
- [ ] do homework
- [ ] play soccer
- [ ] surf the Net
- [ ] go roller-skating
- [ ] listen to music
- [ ] watch TV

**BEN**
- [ ] hang out with friends
- [ ] play computer games
- [ ] do homework
- [ ] read a book
- [ ] go roller-skating
- [ ] go shopping
- [ ] listen to music

**3** Work in pairs. Talk about your day.

A What do you do on Saturday afternoons?

B Well, first I listen to music.

# Grammar

## Simple present Negative

**1** Look at the dialogue on page 70 and complete the table.

| Simple present | Negative |
|---|---|
| I/you/we/they | ¹................. like them. |
| He/she/it | ²................. likes me. |

**2** Rewrite the sentences using the negative form.

1 I like tomatoes.
   *I don't like tomatoes.*
2 He hates soccer.
   ....................................................
3 We know the answer.
   ....................................................
4 You tell good jokes.
   ....................................................
5 They live here.
   ....................................................
6 My brother watches TV every day.
   ....................................................
7 Nicole goes shopping on Fridays.
   ....................................................
8 Our teacher does homework.
   ....................................................

**3** Write the negative form of the verb to complete the sentences.

1 I *don't speak* Spanish. (speak)
2 We ..................... meat on Fridays. (eat)
3 My father ..................... ice cream. (like)
4 They ..................... TV at the weekend. (watch)
5 I'm sorry. I ..................... (understand)
6 Steve ..................... the Net. (surf)
7 She ..................... the answer. (know)
8 Adrian and Mary ..................... in a big house. (live)

## Simple present Questions and short answers

**4** Look at the dialogue on page 70 and complete the table.

| Questions | | |
|---|---|---|
| ¹........... | I/you/we/they | get up at six? |
| **Does** | he/she/it | go to bed at nine o'clock? |

| Short answers | | |
|---|---|---|
| **Affirmative** | Yes, I/you/we/they **do**. | |
| | Yes, he/she/it **does**. | |
| **Negative** | No, I/you/we/they **don't**. | |
| | No, he/she/it **doesn't**. | |

**5** Write questions and short answers.

1 he / play football? (Y)
   *Does he play football*?
   *Yes, he does.*
2 they / watch TV on Fridays? (N)
   ....................................................?
   ....................................................
3 you / eat fruit? (Y)
   ....................................................?
   ....................................................
4 she / go shopping on the weekend? (N)
   ....................................................?
   ....................................................
5 Steve and Nicole / speak Italian? (N)
   ....................................................?
   ....................................................
6 you / like romantic movies? (N)
   ....................................................?
   ....................................................

UNIT 6

**Get talking** Talking about daily routines

**6** Listen to the interview with Nick and Melanie. Draw the time they do each activity on the clocks below.

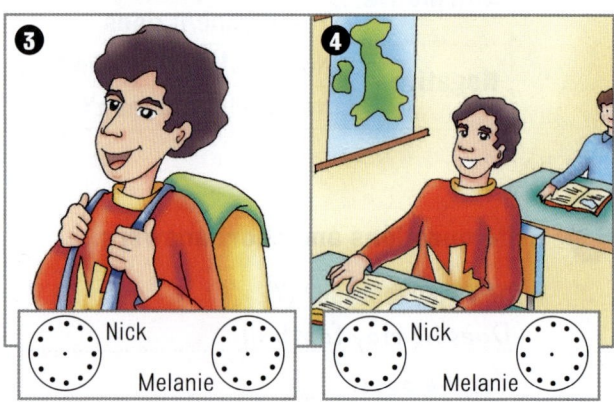

## Object pronouns

**7** Use the words below to complete the table.

him  them  us  me
her  you  it

| Object pronouns | |
|---|---|
| Subject pronoun | Object pronoun |
| I → | 1 .................. |
| you → | 2 .................. |
| he → | 3 .................. |
| she → | 4 .................. |
| it → | 5 .................. |
| we → | 6 .................. |
| they → | 7 .................. |

**8** Circle the correct object pronoun to complete the sentences.

1 This is Mark. Do you know *him* / *her*?
2 They are Chinese. I speak to *them* / *it* every day.
3 That's my house. Do you like *it* / *her*?
4 I'm Maria. Talk to *me* / *him*.
5 We are Japanese, but my American friend lives with *us* / *them*.

**9** Complete with the correct object pronoun.

1 This is my new computer. Do you like ...*it*...?
2 There's Steve. Let's talk to .................. .
3 We play soccer every Sunday. Come and play with ..................!
4 Jennifer Aniston's on TV. Do you like ..................?
5 I go to bed at 10, so please call .................. before then.

# Skills

## Reading

**1** Read the text.

### A Day in the Life of Christina and Suresh

**Hi, I'm Christina.** I live on a farm in Texas. I get up at seven thirty in the morning. At a quarter to eight, I go and feed my horse. At a quarter past eight, I have breakfast with my family. At twenty to nine, my mom drives me to school. School starts at nine o'clock. School ends at four o'clock. My mom picks me up and then we often go shopping. When I come home, I ride my horse for an hour. Then I do my homework or watch TV. Our family has dinner at seven thirty. Then I call my friends or work on my computer. Before I go to sleep, I read for half an hour. I go to bed at ten o'clock or ten thirty.

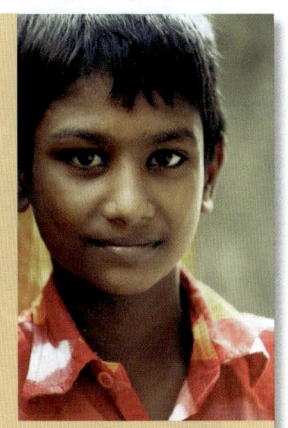

**I'm Suresh.** I live with my mother in a village in India. The big city is six hours away by bus. My mother and I get up at five o'clock in the morning. My mother goes out to cut grass for our water buffalos. I get water from the river. At six o'clock, I make breakfast for my baby brother and mother. At six thirty, I leave for school. I walk to school from six thirty to eight o'clock. School begins at eight o'clock and ends at two thirty. I walk home and then I go out to cut grass for the buffalos. Then I clean the buffalo shed. We go to bed early, usually at eight thirty or nine o'clock.

**2** Put a check next to the correct times for the activities.

1. Christina gets up at .......... .
   a □   b □   c □

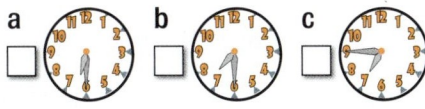

2. Suresh gets up at .......... .
   a □   b □   c □

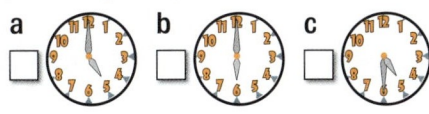

3. At .......... Christina has breakfast.
   a □   b □   c □

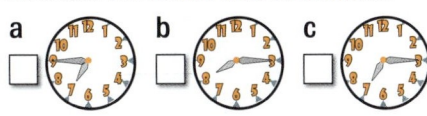

4. At .......... Suresh makes breakfast.
   a □   b □   c □

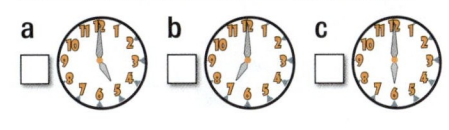

5. At .......... Christina goes to school.
   a □   b □   c □

6. Suresh leaves for school at .......... .
   a □   b □   c □

7. Christina's family has dinner at .......... .
   a □   b □   c □

8. Suresh's school ends at .......... .
   a □   b □   c □

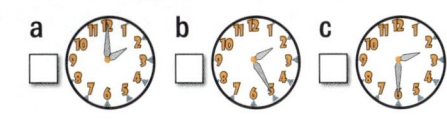

## A Song 4 U  The master of time

**3** Listen and complete. Then sing.

o'clock
quarter
Ten to (x 3)
twelve
clock (x 2)

The master of time!

I'm the master, the
master of time. (x 2)

Chorus (x 2)
Listen, I'm
the master of time, (x 2)
and here's my rhyme.

Six ¹..................,
let's play some rock.
Ten past eight—uh oh,
I'm late.
² .................. three,
slap your knee.
From ³ .................. to one,
let's have some fun.

I'm the master,
the master of time (x 2)

One to three, rock with me
a ⁴.................. past,
this is too fast.
⁵.................. ten,
and this is when
I hear a knock my good old ⁶.................. .

Chorus

⁷.................. 10, and this is when
I hear a knock my good old
⁸.................. . (x 2)
One last hop, we have to stop.

Chorus (x 1)

Listen, I'm the master of time,
the master of time and here, my friend,
is the end, of my rhyme, my rhyme.
Oh, yeah, baby!

# Writing for your Portfolio

**4** Read the text and describe your day.

### A day in the life of Sarah Brown

I get up at seven. I have breakfast at a quarter past seven. I go to school at a quarter to eight. Our school starts at eight o'clock and it ends at twelve thirty. In the afternoon, I play with my friends, read, or listen to music. Then I do my homework. I often watch TV from six to eight. At nine o'clock I go to bed.

MORE fun with Fido

# Check your progress Units 5 and 6

**1** Write two words for each category.

1 vegetables ......................................
2 drinks ......................................
3 fruit ......................................
4 meat ......................................

☐ 8

**2** Put the sentences in order to form a dialogue.

.......... I'd like a steak, please.
.......... What would you like to eat?
.......... No, thanks. I don't like them.
.......... May I have potatoes?
.......... Of course. Would you like carrots, too?
.......... What vegetables would you like?

☐ 6

**3** Put a check next to the correct sentences, and correct the ones that are wrong.

1 I eat fruit never. ☐
...........................................................

2 They always go to bed at ten o'clock. ☐
...........................................................

3 My teacher often is late for class. ☐
...........................................................

4 We sometimes go to the movies with Jack. ☐
...........................................................

5 He watches usually TV after dinner. ☐
...........................................................

☐ 5

**4** Rewrite the sentences using the negative form.

1 I go to the gym every day.
...........................................................

2 Sue and Belinda like ice cream.
...........................................................

3 Nicole wants chicken and french fries.
...........................................................

4 My mother drinks a lot of coffee.
...........................................................

5 School finishes at four o'clock.
...........................................................

☐ 10

**5** Match the words.

1 play           a shopping
2 listen         b the dog
3 hang out       c a book
4 go             d to music
5 read           e TV
6 watch          f the piano
7 walk           g with friends

☐ 7

**6** Complete the dialogues with object pronouns.

1 **A** Do you want to watch *Glee* tonight?
  **B** No, thanks. I don't like ..................... .
2 **A** Would you like to talk to Charles?
  **B** Yes, I would. Let's call ..................... .
3 **A** Are you home tonight?
  **B** Yes. Call ..................... at nine o'clock.
4 **A** Why don't you have dogs at your house?
  **B** Because we don't like ..................... .

☐ 4

**7** Answer the questions.

1 What time do you get up?
...........................................................

2 When does school start?
...........................................................

3 Do you take the bus to school?
...........................................................

4 Do you have homework every day?
...........................................................

5 Do you play a sport after school?
...........................................................

☐ 10

**TOTAL** ☐ 50

---

**My progress so far is...**

☺ great!  ☐
😐 good.   ☐
☹ poor.   ☐

# Multicultural America

**1** Match the countries to the correct languages.

| | | | |
|---|---|---|---|
| 1 | France | a | Spanish |
| 2 | Iran | b | Vietnamese |
| 3 | Turkey | c | Greek |
| 4 | Brazil & Portugal | d | Albanian |
| 5 | Canada | e | French |
| 6 | Vietnam | f | Turkish |
| 7 | Spain & Mexico | g | Farsi |
| 8 | Egypt | h | Arabic |
| 9 | Albania | i | Portuguese |
| 10 | Greece | j | French & English |

## FACT FILE

### FOCUS ON CALIFORNIA

People from all around the world live in California. **Sacramento** is the capital city of California. It is known as America's most diverse city. People living there speak as many as 150 different languages.

**Common languages**

Spanish   Turkish   Polish   French   Hmong
English   Portuguese   Hindi   Mien   Greek   Spanish
Vietnamese   Mandarin   Cantonese

**2** Read the texts and answer the questions.

**TALKING ABOUT MUSIC**

NAME Gursharan Singh
NATIONALITY Indian
HOME Sacramento

Bhangra music is growing in popularity in Sacramento. Bhangra is a new trend in dance music but it is originally a folk dance from Punjab in India. Modern Bhangra is a mixture of hip-hop, reggae, house, and drum-and-bass. My favorite musicians are Missy Elliot, Jazzy Bains, and Punjabi MC.

NAME Zeynep Aksu
NATIONALITY Turkish
HOME Sacramento

Turkish pop music is big in the Turkish community here. It has a different sound from other pop music. It's a mixture of Eastern and Western music. My favorite pop singer is Tarkan. He's gorgeous! Rafet el Roman, Sertab Erener, and Aşkın Nur Yengi are good singers, too.

1  What sort of music is Bhangra?
2  What is Turkish pop music like?
3  Where is Bhangra from originally?
4  Who is Tarkan?

**3** Listen to the interview and complete the text.

**Name** Manuel Bautista   **Nationality** Mexican   **Home** Sacramento

Manuel is from ¹.................. but his family is from ².................. . His favorite ³.................. is salsa. Salsa ⁴.................. popular in Sacramento. It is ⁵.................. and it has got a strong dance beat. His ⁶.................. musician is his dad. He is a ⁷.................. in a salsa band. There are a lot of salsa ⁸.................. in California. Salsa music and dance are very popular.

**4** **Over 2 U!** Interview a partner and write a paragraph about his or her favorite music.

**MORE!** Now you can watch Episode 6 of *The Story of the Stones*.

78 UNIT 6

# The world's best detective

**Detective Case** is at home. The telephone rings.

"Hello, this is Detective Case, the world's best detective."

"This is Penelope Gray. Can you help me find my cat, Pepper? I don't know where he is."

"Don't worry, Miss Gray."

Detective Case leaves his house. He looks for Pepper. He comes to a bridge.

"Maybe Pepper is under the bridge."

He looks under the bridge. Pepper isn't there. Case falls into the river.

Detective Case goes to the park. He looks for Pepper, but he bumps into a tree.

"Maybe Pepper is in the park."

"OK. Maybe Pepper is in the woods."

Detective Case goes into the woods. He looks for Pepper, but he sees a wolf!

Detective Case climbs a tree and waits. He watches the wolf. He's very scared. He hears a noise. He looks around, and he sees—Pepper!

Detective Case is very happy. He picks Pepper up and calls Penelope Gray.

"Hello? Miss Gray? I'm in the woods. I have Pepper."

"Wonderful!"

"But I have a problem. There's a wolf here. Please help me!"

"Give me 2 minutes!"

For **MORE!** Go to www.more-online.com/american to check the ending of the story. Then take a quiz on this text.

# American MORE! 1A

**Herbert Puchta & Jeff Stranks**
G. Gerngross  C. Holzmann  P. Lewis-Jones

## COMBO Workbook

# CONTENTS

**UNIT 1** Hello! — page 84

**UNIT 2** In the classroom — page 90

**UNIT 3** My bedroom — page 96

**UNIT 4** Who's that boy? — page 102

**UNIT 5** What's for lunch? — page 108

**UNIT 6** Time for a change — page 114

Grammar Review — page 123

① **Complete the dialogue using the words below.**

I'm   Nice to meet you   thanks   This is   Hi   Vicky

❶ Hi, Ashley. How are you?

1 .................... , Andrew.
2 .................... fine,
3 ....................

❷ Hi Vicky.
4 ....................
Nicole.

Hello Nicole.
6 ....................
....................

Hi, 5 ....................

② **Complete the dialogues.**

❶ Hi, I'm James and this is Claire.

❷ Hello, ....................
....................

❸ ....................
....................

❹ .................... and this is my ....................

84 UNIT 1

# Language Focus

## Vocabulary Feelings

**1** Write a word to describe the emotion of each person.

1. _happy_
2. ..................
3. ..................
4. ..................
5. ..................
6. ..................
7. ..................
8. ..................
9. ..................
10. ..................

**2** Write six short dialogues about the people in Exercise 1.

A _Who's happy?_
B _Karl._

A ..................
B ..................

A ..................
B ..................

A ..................
B ..................

A ..................
B ..................

A ..................
B ..................

UNIT 1 85

# Grammar

## Simple present of *be* Affirmative

**1** Complete the sentences. Use the affirmative short form.

1. Pablo and Juanita .................. from Santiago, Chile.
2. I .................. cold!
3. You .................. right.
4. Jenny .................. 13.

## Simple present of *be* Negative

**2** Rewrite the sentences. Use the negative short form.

1. She is not English.
   *She isn't English.*

2. They are not OK.
   ..................

3. You are not nice.
   ..................

4. He is not hungry.
   ..................

5. We are not sad.
   ..................

6. I am not late.
   ..................

**3** Complete the sentences. Use the negative short form.

1. I *'m not* angry. I'm sad.
2. She .................. wrong. She's right.
3. They .................. Mexican. They're Guatemalan.
4. We .................. 12. We're 13.
5. He .................. happy. He's angry.
6. It .................. my sandwich. It's yours.

**4** Look at the pictures and complete the sentences.

1. James isn't happy. He's *angry*.
2. Sara .................. 10. .................. 11. 
3. Juan .................. thirsty. He .................. 
4. Maria .................. cold. She .................. 
5. Serena and Mark .................. happy. They .................. 
6. Ronin and Liza .................. 11. They ..................

## Simple present of *be* Questions and short answers

**5** Complete the questions and short answers.

1 ...*Is*... Jenny Canadian?
No, she isn't.

2 .............. it Aliana's dog?
Yes, it ..............

3 .............. Steve sixteen?
No, he ..............

4 .............. they hungry?
Yes, they ..............

5 .............. you nervous?
Yes, I ..............

6 .............. we late?
Yes, you ..............

## Questions with *Who...?*

**6** Match the question to the correct answer.

1 Who's your English teacher?
2 Who are your best friends?
3 Who's your favorite actor?
4 Who are you?
5 Who are Ken and Liz?
6 Who's hungry?

a Brad Pitt. He's so cool.
b I'm Matt.
c I am.
d Mark and Laura.
e It's Mrs. Simmons. She's very nice.
f Ken and Liz? They're in my class.

## Possessive adjectives Review

**7** Complete the sentences with *my*, *your*, *his*, *her*, or *their*.

1 ...*Is*... it your cat?
Yes, ...*it is*...

2 ..............?
No, ..............

3 ..............?
No, ..............

4 ..............?
No, ..............

5 ..............?
Yes, ..............

6 ..............?
No, ..............

UNIT 1 87

# Skills

## Listening

**1 Listen and complete.**

① Dawn is .................. .

② A .................., please. ..................

③ The hamburger's .................. .

④ Dawn is still .................. . Now she is .................. .

⑤

⑥ Now Dawn is .................. .

⑦ .................. . Yum!

⑧ Dawn isn't .................. now. She's sick.

**2 Complete the dialogue.**

**Tom** Hi, Sue.
**Sue** ¹.................. , Tom. How ²..................?
**Tom** ³.................. fine. And you?
**Sue** I'm ⁴.................. .
**Tom** Angry? Why? What's the problem?
**Sue** Look! My MP3 player.
**Tom** Oh, ⁵.................. so sorry, Sue.

## Listening

**3** Write the sentences under the correct pictures. Then listen to the story and put the pictures in the correct order.

Flozza's hungry.   Mary and Kate are happy.   Kate's angry.   Flozza's happy.

## Reading

**4** Read Tim's diary, decide if the sentences are T (True) or F (False), and circle the correct answer.

**Monday** It's Monday evening. I'm very happy. A great day at school. And a good movie on TV!

**Tuesday** I'm so angry. A lot of homework!

**Wednesday** I'm nervous. There's a test on Friday.

**Thursday** Today I'm OK. Chicken for dinner, my favorite!

**Friday** I'm not angry today. And I'm not sad. I'm happy. Great test!

**Saturday and Sunday** Cool weekend. I'm very happy. :)

1  On Monday Tim is happy.                                             T / F
2  On Tuesday he is angry and nervous.                                 T / F
3  On Wednesday he is nervous. There's a test on Thursday!             T / F
4  On Thursday he is not OK.                                           T / F
5  On Friday he is angry.                                              T / F
6  On Saturday and Sunday he is very happy.                            T / F

**1** **Write the sentences in the correct cartoons.**

Pick it up.
Be quiet.
Don't laugh.
Don't put it on my desk.
Open your books.
Sit next to me.
Sit down.
Stand up.

**2** **Complete the questions and the answers. Use the prepositions *next to*, *under*, *on*, *in*, *in front of*, and *behind*.**

1 Where are the books?
   *They're in* the box.
2 Where's the bike?
   .................... the table.
3 .................... the cat?
   .................... the TV.
4 .................... the sandwiches?
   .................... the bed.
5 .................... the banana?
   .................... the floor.
6 .................... the hamster?
   .................... the bike.
7 .................... the light?
   .................... the bed.
8 .................... the sandwiches?
   .................... the banana.

90 UNIT 2

# Language Focus

## Vocabulary Classroom objects

**1** Listen and color the objects.

## Saying where things are

**2** Write questions and answers about the objects above.

1. chairs / desks
   A *Where are the chairs?*
   B *They're under the desks.*

2. laptop / interactive white board
   A ..........................................................
   B ..........................................................

3. books / desks
   A ..........................................................
   B ..........................................................

4. computer / window
   A ..........................................................
   B ..........................................................

5. table / computer
   A ..........................................................
   B ..........................................................

6. interactive white board / laptop
   A ..........................................................
   B ..........................................................

7. window / computer
   A ..........................................................
   B ..........................................................

8. CD player / door
   A ..........................................................
   B ..........................................................

## Sounds right /ə/

**3** Listen and circle the /ə/ sound.

1. teacher    2. color    3. father    4. doctor    5. sister

# Grammar

## Imperatives

**1** Complete the imperatives. Then write them in the negative form.

> down  ~~up~~  in pairs  your books
> the window  quiet

1 Stand ...up!...  Don't stand up!
2 Open ........................  ........................
3 Sit ........................  ........................
4 Be ........................  ........................
5 Close ........................  ........................
6 Work ........................  ........................

**2** Write the correct phrase under the picture.

> Sit down, please.  Don't look!  Stand up.
> Sit next to me, Tom.  Pick it up.  Look!

1 ........................
2 ........................ 
3 ........................ 
4 ........................ 
5 ........................ 
6 ........................  

**3** Complete the sentences with these words.

> open  sit  don't open  don't be
> stand  come

1 ........................ angry.

2 It's so hot here. Please ........................ the window.

3 ........................ out!

4 ........................ the gate!

5 ........................ here!

6 ........................ up, please.

## Questions with Who? / Where? / Why? / What? / What color?

**4** Write the correct question word.

1. **A** ........................'s your favorite singer?
   **B** Rhianna.
2. **A** ........................'s your favorite sport?
   **B** Football.
3. **A** ........................'s *"verde"* in English?
   **B** It's "green."
4. **A** ........................'s your father's car?
   **B** It's red.
5. **A** ........................ are you under the desk?
   **B** My book's on the floor.
6. **A** ........................'s Sandra?
   **B** She's at school.

**5** Reorder the words and write questions.

1. their / names / are / what
   *What are their names?*
2. your / singer / who / favorite / is
   ........................
3. happy / why / are / so / you
   ........................
4. your / English book / where / is
   ........................
5. color / your / what / is / backpack
   ........................
6. your / is / English teacher / who
   ........................

**6** Write questions using *what, where, why, who,* or *how old.*

1. ........................?
   It's blue.
2. ........................?
   They're red and blue.
3. ........................?
   He's my best friend.
4. ........................?
   They're on your desk.
5. ........................?
   She's in her car.
6. ........................?
   My dog's not here.
7. ........................?
   It's pizza.
8. ........................?
   She's 12 years old.

**7** Write personal answers to the questions.

1. What color is your backpack?
   ........................
2. Who's your favorite singer?
   ........................
5. How old are you?
   ........................
3. What's your favorite colour?
   ........................
4. Who's your English teacher?
   ........................
6. Where's your school?
   ........................

UNIT 2 93

# Skills

## Reading

**1** Read the interview.

## music scene Profiles
### Lead singer James from Project 11

**Music Scene:** This week, we're with a new band from Austin, Texas. Their name's Project 11, and James Brooks is the lead singer.

**James:** That's right, I'm the lead singer for Project 11. But don't forget, Project 11 has six people! The other five people in the band are Jessica, Jack, Ellie, Dan, and Steve.

**Music Scene:** OK. And how old are you all?

**James:** Well, I'm 16. Jessica, Ellie, and Dan are 16, too. Steve and Jack are 17.

**Music Scene:** And are you all from Austin?

**James:** No, we aren't. Dan and Steve are from San Antonio. But Ellie, Jessica, Jack, and I are from Austin.

**Music Scene:** I see. And James, what star sign are you?

**James:** I'm a Scorpio. My birthday's November 12.

**Music Scene:** Who are your favorite bands and singers?

**James:** Well, my favorite band is U2. And my favorite singer's Bono. But don't ask me about the others in Project 11!

**Music Scene:** OK. And what's your favorite animal, day of the week, color, and number?

**James:** Wow! Um, cats, Saturday, black, and 13. Lucky 13!

**Music Scene:** James Brooks, thanks a lot.

**James:** You're welcome. And thank you.

**2** Decide if the sentences are T (True) or F (False).

1  Project 11 are from Dallas.   T / F
2  James is lead singer for Project 11.   T / F
3  The six people in the band are 15 years old.   T / F
4  James is from Austin.   T / F
5  His star sign is Scorpio.   T / F
6  His favorite band is Project 11.   T / F
7  Cats are his favorite animal.   T / F
8  Twelve is his favorite number.   T / F

**3** Complete the table for James.

| Name | Age | From |
|---|---|---|
| Star sign | Favorite band | |
| Favorite animal | Favorite color | |

## Listening

**4** Listen and complete the table for Jessica.

| Name | | Age | From |
|---|---|---|---|
| Star sign | Gemini | Favorite band | |
| Favorite animal | | Favorite color | |

## Writing for your Portfolio

**5** Complete the table for a friend.

| Name | Age | From |
|---|---|---|
| Star sign | Favorite band | |
| Favorite animal | Favorite color | |

## Listening

**6** Listen and put a check next to the correct picture.

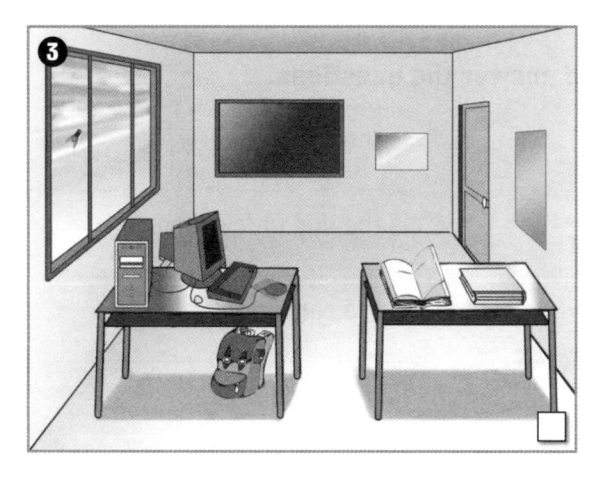

UNIT 2 95

# UNIT 3 My bedroom

**1** Complete the sentences using the adjectives below.

> new   old   big   friendly   small   early   unfriendly   late

1  An ..................... cat.
2  An ..................... bike. 
3  A ..................... ice cream. 
4  A ..................... pizza slice. 
5  A ..................... teacher. 
6  A ..................... dog. 
7  A ..................... car. 
8  An ..................... student. 

**2** Look at the pictures in Exercise 1 and answer the questions.

1  Is the cat friendly?
   *No, it's unfriendly.*
2  Is the bike new?
   ........................................................
3  Is the ice cream small?
   ........................................................
4  Is the pizza slice big?
   ........................................................
5  Is the teacher early?
   ........................................................
6  Is the dog unfriendly?
   ........................................................
7  Is the car old?
   ........................................................
8  Is the student late?
   ........................................................

# Language Focus

## Vocabulary Furniture

**1** Write the correct word under the picture.

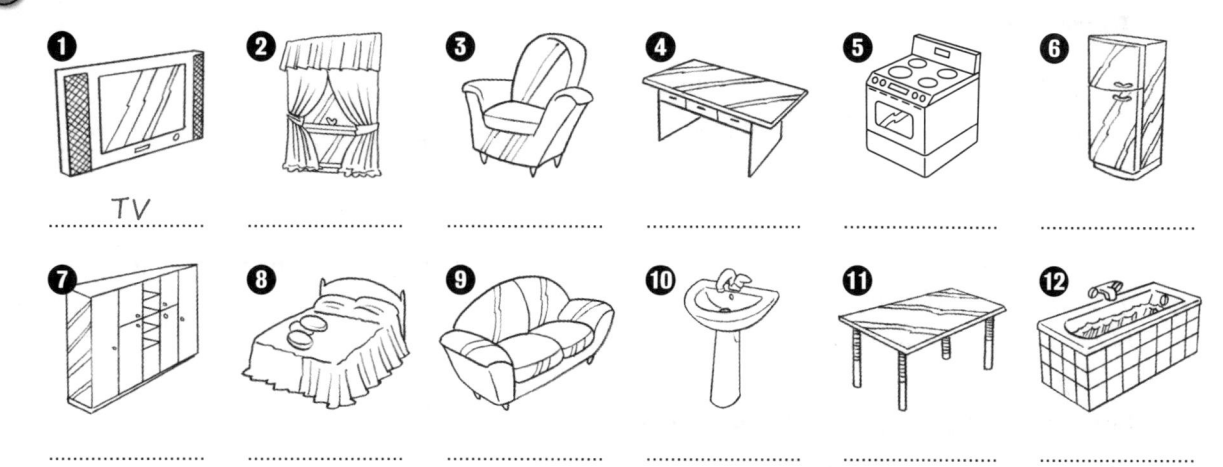

1. TV
2. ..........
3. ..........
4. ..........
5. ..........
6. ..........
7. ..........
8. ..........
9. ..........
10. ..........
11. ..........
12. ..........

**2** Write the name of each room.

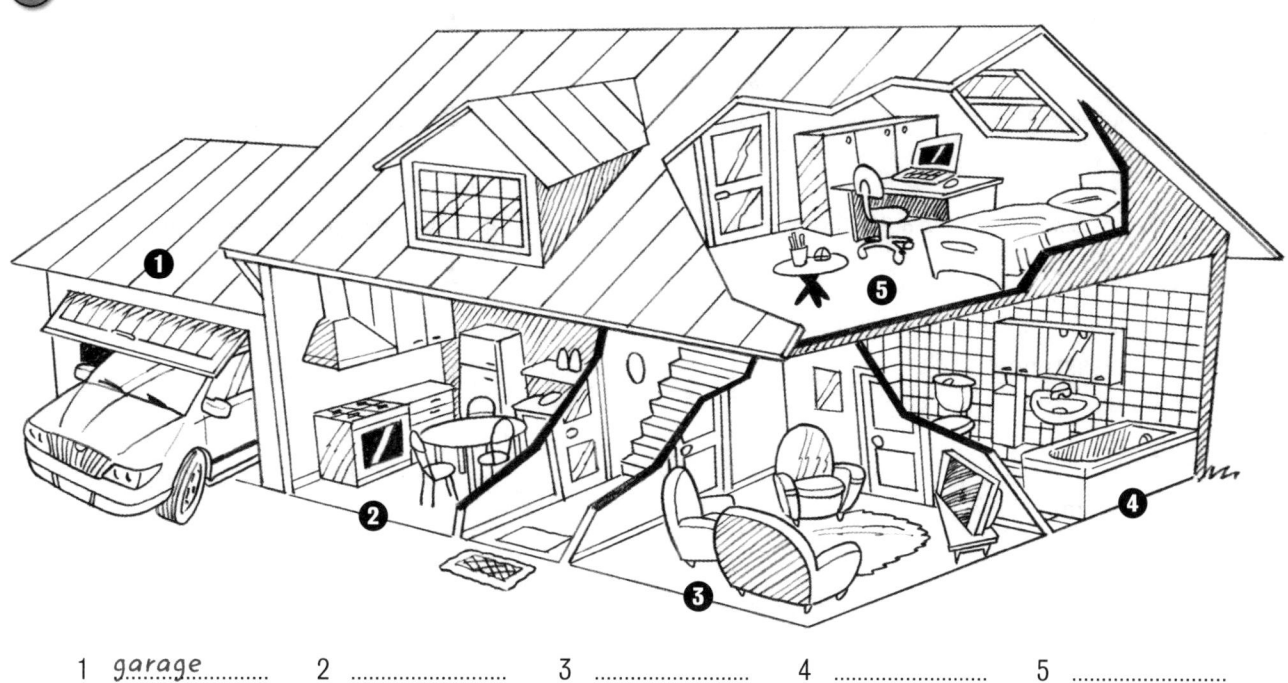

1 *garage*   2 ..........   3 ..........   4 ..........   5 ..........

## Talking about rooms and furniture

**3** Write sentences about your living room, kitchen, and bedroom.

1 In the living room, there's a sofa and there are two ..........................................
..................................................................................................................................
2 In the ............................................................................................................................
..................................................................................................................................
3 In the ............................................................................................................................
..................................................................................................................................

UNIT 3 97

# Grammar

## There is / are

**1** Complete the sentences with *There's* or *There are*.

1 ...*There's*... a CD player on the table.
2 ..................... five children in the car.
3 ..................... a fly on the window.
4 ..................... a picture of a frog on my T-shirt.
5 ..................... 10 books in the bag.
6 ..................... three DVDs on my desk.

**2** Complete the sentences with the correct form of *there is* or *there are*.

1 ...*Is there*... a TV in your bedroom?
Yes, there is.
2 ..................... a lot of apples in the kitchen?
No, .....................
3 ..................... a good movie on TV?
Yes, .....................
4 ..................... a computer in your classroom?
No, .....................
5 ..................... two bookshelves in your room?
Yes, .....................
6 ..................... a lot of people at your party?
Yes, .....................
7 ..................... a math test tomorrow?
No, .....................

**3** Write the dialogues using the words below.

1 a blue pencil case in your bag / green
A *Is there a blue pencil case in your bag?*
B *No, there isn't. There's a green pencil case.*

2 five CDs on the table / three
A .....................
B .....................

3 a man in the yard / a woman
A .....................
B .....................

4 six books in that bag / seven
A .....................
B .....................

5 a lot of cars on the street / one car
A .....................
B .....................

6 19 children in your class / 21
A .....................
B .....................

## Adjectives

**4** Reorder the words and write the sentences.

1. TV / big / a / there's
   *There's a big TV.*

2. city / beautiful / a / Rome / is
   ............................................

3. student / Sarah / new / a / is
   ............................................

4. good / a / he / friend / is
   ............................................

5. dog / it's / friendly / a
   ............................................

6. 10 / are / desks / small / there
   ............................................

7. new / four / there / cars / are
   ............................................

8. great / a / song / is / this
   ............................................

9. are / two / pizzas / there / big
   ............................................

10. MP3 player / pink / it's / a
    ............................................

## Possessives

**5** Read the sentences below and put a check in the correct column. Is the *'s* a possessive or the short form of *is*?

|   | | Possessive | is |
|---|---|---|---|
| 1 | My friend's from New York. | ☐ | ☐ |
| 2 | Peter's new car is black. | ☐ | ☐ |
| 3 | Spaghetti's my favorite food. | ☐ | ☐ |
| 4 | What's the problem? | ☐ | ☐ |
| 5 | Joshua's ideas are great. | ☐ | ☐ |
| 6 | I think Sue is Amanda's friend. | ☐ | ☐ |
| 7 | Richard's a great guy! | ☐ | ☐ |
| 8 | Who's your favorite singer? | ☐ | ☐ |

**6** Rewrite the sentences. Substitute the possessive adjective with the name in parentheses.

1. Please give me his phone number. (Tony)
   *Please give me Tony's phone number.*

2. Are there a lot of posters in her room? (Sandra)
   ............................................

3. His jeans are under the bed. (Tom)
   ............................................

4. Is she her new friend? (Alison)
   ............................................

5. Steak is his favorite food. (Christopher)
   ............................................

6. Is it her book? (Elisabeth)
   ............................................

7. Her school is in Texas. (Samantha)
   ............................................

8. Is his friend nice? (Michael)
   ............................................

9. There's a TV in his room. (Luke)
   ............................................

10. Where's her house? (Tessa)
    ............................................

# Skills

## Reading

**1** Read Lucy's letter. Write the names of the correct animals under the photos.

Dear Melissa,

Hi from the National Zoo in Washington, D.C. There are so many interesting animals here. There are a lot of pandas and three Asian elephants. One of the elephants was born in 2001. His name is Kandula, and he's so sweet.

There is a lush rain forest walk known as Amazonia. There is a large Great Ape House with six gorillas. There are also a lot of snakes and there's even a Komodo dragon!

And there's a good café with delicious ice cream!

Your friend, Lucy

This is me. I'm scared!

The café is great!

1 snake   2   3   4   5

**2** Reread Lucy's letter and decide if the sentences below are T (True) or F (False).

1  Lucy is at the National Zoo.                T / F
2  There is a kangaroo.                        T / F
3  There are four elephants.                   T / F
4  The koalas are from Asia.                   T / F
5  There is an elephant born in 2001.          T / F
6  The youngest elephant's name is Hans.       T / F
7  There is a rain forest walk.                T / F
8  There are a lot of snakes.                  T / F
9  There's a café.                             T / F
10 The ice cream is not very good.             T / F

**3** Read the email and match the sentence halves below.

Hello Andrew,
This is a picture of my new bedroom. It's not very big. There's a bed, desk, and chair. There are two windows. The curtains are blue. On the desk there is a computer and a photo of my dog, Blackie. There are six posters in my room. There are animals on all the posters, including two crocodiles, gorillas, elephants from Africa, snakes, and pelicans. The posters are beautiful.
Best wishes,
Daniel

1 In Daniel's room
2 Daniel's room
3 There are two windows with blue
4 There's a computer on
5 Daniel's pet is
6 The dog's name
7 There are posters
8 On the posters there are

a Daniel's desk.
b there's a bed, desk, and chair.
c a dog.
d is not very big.
e a lot of animals.
f in Daniel's room.
g is Blackie.
h curtains.

## Listening

**4** Listen to the description of Judy's bedroom and check the correct picture.

# Writing for your Portfolio

**5** Think of your ideal bedroom and describe it.

In my new bedroom there's

# UNIT 4 Who's that boy?

**1** Look at the pictures and complete the dialogue.

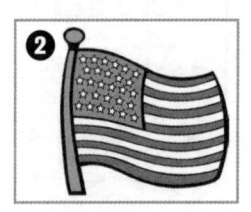

A There's a new ¹..................... in my class.
B Oh really?
A Yeah, she's ²......................
B How old is she?
A She's ³......................
B Is she ⁴...................... ?
A Yes, she is, and she has ⁵...................... hair and brown ⁶......................

**2** Look at the pictures and answer the questions.

1 Who's Japanese? .....Haro.....
2 Who's Brazilian? ......................
3 Who has a computer?
   ......................
4 Who has short hair? ......................
5 Who has long hair? ......................
6 Who has a car? ......................

**3** Write sentences about the people in Exercise 2 using the questions above.

1 <u>Haro is Japanese. He has short hair. He's</u> ......................
2 <u>Fernanda's</u> ......................

**4** Answer the questions about yourself. Write Yes or No.

1 Are you Japanese?        <u>Yes/No</u>
2 Are you 13?              ............
3 Do you have black hair?  ............
4 Do you have brown eyes?  ............
5 Do you have a bicycle?            ............
6 Do you have a dog?                ............
7 Does your family have a big house? ............
8 Do you have a computer in your bedroom? ............

## Sounds right /h/

**5a** Listen and circle the word you hear.

1 hair  air    2 hungry  angry    3 hand  and    4 his  is    5 ham  am

**5b** Listen and write the sentences.

1 ......................
2 ......................

# Language Focus

## Vocabulary  Countries and nationalities

**1** Find and circle 12 countries. Then write them with the correct nationality.

```
J A P A N I C W E F G E
S D E I P T R H I R E L
Z C O L M A A U I A R A
B R A Z I L N S A L N I
T U R K E Y D R G C E M
A U S R T E G R E E C E
C O L O M B I A R A H X
N F X P O L E K M B I I
P O C A N A D A A C N C
M A R I I T C A N D A O
I N D I A S A S Y R I W
```

1. Italy — Italian
2. ..................... — .....................
3. ..................... — .....................
4. ..................... — .....................
5. ..................... — .....................
6. ..................... — .....................
7. ..................... — .....................
8. ..................... — .....................
9. ..................... — .....................
10. ..................... — .....................
11. ..................... — .....................
12. ..................... — .....................

## Vocabulary  Parts of the body

**2** Find 12 parts of the body in the wordsnake below and write them in the correct place on the picture.

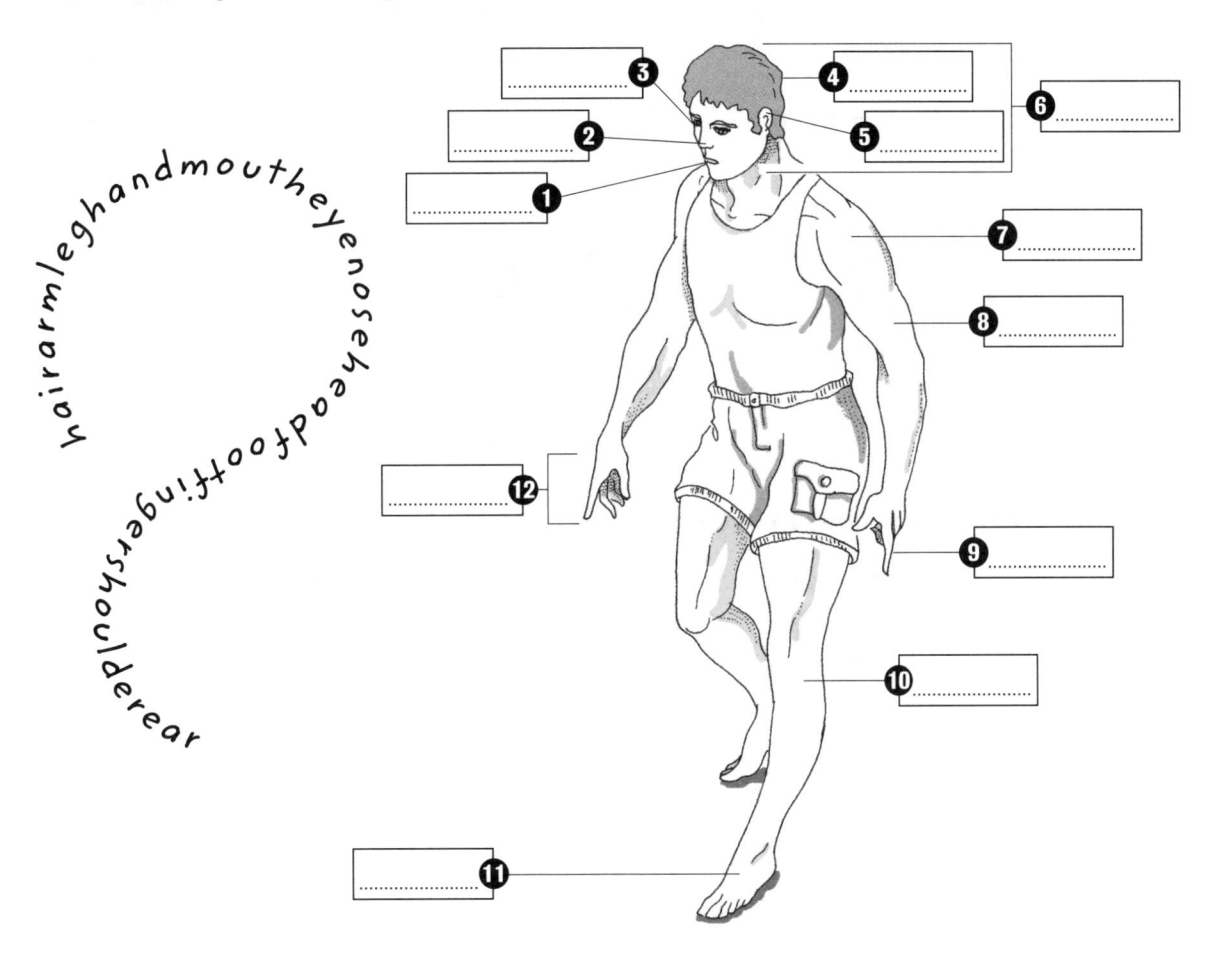

hairarmleghandmoutheyenoseheadfootfingershoulderear

# Grammar

## have / has

**1** Complete the table.

| I | 1 have | |
|---|---|---|
| You | 2 .......... | |
| He/She/It | 3 .......... | black hair. |
| We | 4 .......... | |
| You | 5 .......... | |
| They | 6 .......... | |

**2** Write sentences. Use the affirmative form.

1 She / blonde hair  *She has blonde hair.*
2 They / a new car  ..............................
3 He / a laptop  ..............................
4 She / a cat  ..............................
5 He / long hair  ..............................
6 I / an MP3 player  ..............................

**3** Circle the correct form of the verb.

1 He *don't / doesn't* have long hair.
2 She *don't / doesn't* have a bicycle. 
3 It *don't / doesn't* have long legs. 
4 I *don't / doesn't* have a computer. 
5 We *don't / doesn't* have a big house. 
6 They *don't / doesn't* have hamburgers. 

**4** Rewrite the sentences in the negative form.

1 I have a new bicycle.
   *I don't have a new bicycle.*
2 They have a big house.
   ..............................
3 He has blue eyes.
   ..............................
4 You have brown hair.
   ..............................
5 We have a yellow sofa.
   ..............................
6 I have a cat.
   ..............................

### 5  Reorder the words and write questions.

1 have / a / does / pen / he — Does he have a pen?
2 they / laptop / do / have / a — ...................................................
3 you / problem / have / a / do — ...................................................
4 green / does / she / eyes / have — ...................................................
5 we / have / a / family / big / do — ...................................................
6 he / hair / long / does / have — ...................................................

### 6  Write the questions.

1 I / time? — Do I have time?
2 you / a new computer? — ...................................................
3 she / a big house? — ...................................................
4 we / an Italian car? — ...................................................
5 they / a dog? — ...................................................
6 the dog / long ears? — ...................................................

### 7  Match the answers to the questions from Exercise 6.

a No, you don't. ............
b Yes, they do. ............
c No, she doesn't. ............
d Yes, it does. ............
e Yes, I do. ............
f No, we don't. ............

### 8  Write short answers: (✗) negative and (✓) affirmative.

1 Does he have fair hair? (✗) — No, he doesn't.
2 Do you have a dog? (✓) — ...................................................
3 Does she have a cat? (✗) — ...................................................
4 Do they have a computer in their house? (✗) — ...................................................
5 Do we have homework tonight? (✓) — ...................................................
6 Do they have a big TV? (✓) — ...................................................
7 Does the house have a garage? (✓) — ...................................................
8 Do Mr. and Mrs. Jones have a car? (✗) — ...................................................

## The indefinite article

### 9  Complete with *a* or *an*.

1 She has ...an... apple.
2 Do you have ............ problem?
3 There's ............ fridge in the kitchen.
4 There's ............ armchair in my bedroom.
5 He doesn't have ............ American accent.
6 They have ............ Japanese car.

# Skills

## Listening

**1** Listen and draw the butterfly in the pictures. Then write the sentences.

① ② ③

The butterfly's on ........................

④ ⑤ ⑥

## Reading

**2** Complete the sentences using the words below.

| she's | fair | long | athlete | broad |
| arms | plays | eyes | swimmer | legs |

Vicky Gates is a professional body builder. She has [1]........................, [2]........................ hair and blue eyes. She has long legs and very strong [3]........................ . Vicky is American.

Freda Kapowski [4]........................ professional basketball. She has very long [5]........................ and [6]........................ very tall!

Joanna Mather is an international [7]........................ . She has short, brown hair and green eyes. She may be short, but she has very [8]........................ shoulders.

Jo Kelly is an [9]........................ . She has long, dark hair and blue [10]........................ . She has very long legs. Jo is from Nigeria.

## Listening

**3** **Listen and reorder the phrases to make a dialogue.**

- [ ] And do you have posters in your room?
- [ ] Yeah, he's great. He has blonde hair and green eyes.
- [ ] Kobe Bryant's in it!
- [ ] One or two. My favorite is an L.A. Lakers poster.
- [1] Do you have any posters in your bedroom?
- [ ] Oh? Why?
- [ ] Yes, I do. A lot! My favorite is my poster of Brad Pitt.

## Reading

**4** **Read the paragraph about Alice and correct the sentences.**

This is Alice. She's Brazilian and she's from Rio de Janeiro. She's 16 years old. She has dark hair and brown eyes. She has a small nose. Her favorite colors are red, white, and blue.

1 Alice is Canadian.
   *Brazilian*

2 She's from Buffalo.

3 She's 14.

4 She has blonde hair and brown eyes.

5 Her favorite colors are red and blue.

## Writing for your Portfolio

**5** **Look at the photos and write a paragraph about Jack. Use Exercise 4 as a model.**

# UNIT 5  What's for lunch?

## 1  Look at the pictures and write the correct words.

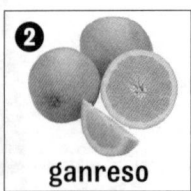

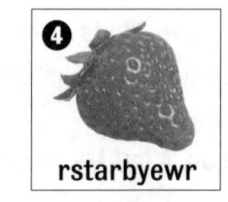

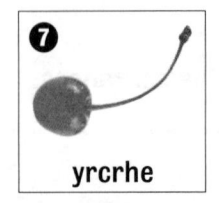

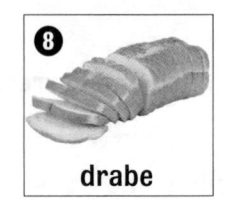

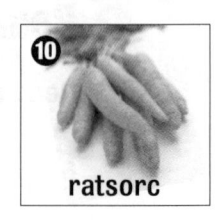

1. anaanb — banana
2. ganreso — ...........
3. geburrsmah — ...........
4. rstarbyewr — ...........
5. inoon — ...........
6. ndaschiw — ...........
7. yrcrhe — ...........
8. drabe — ...........
9. turgoy — ...........
10. ratsorc — ...........

## 2  Follow the lines and write sentences using *like*.

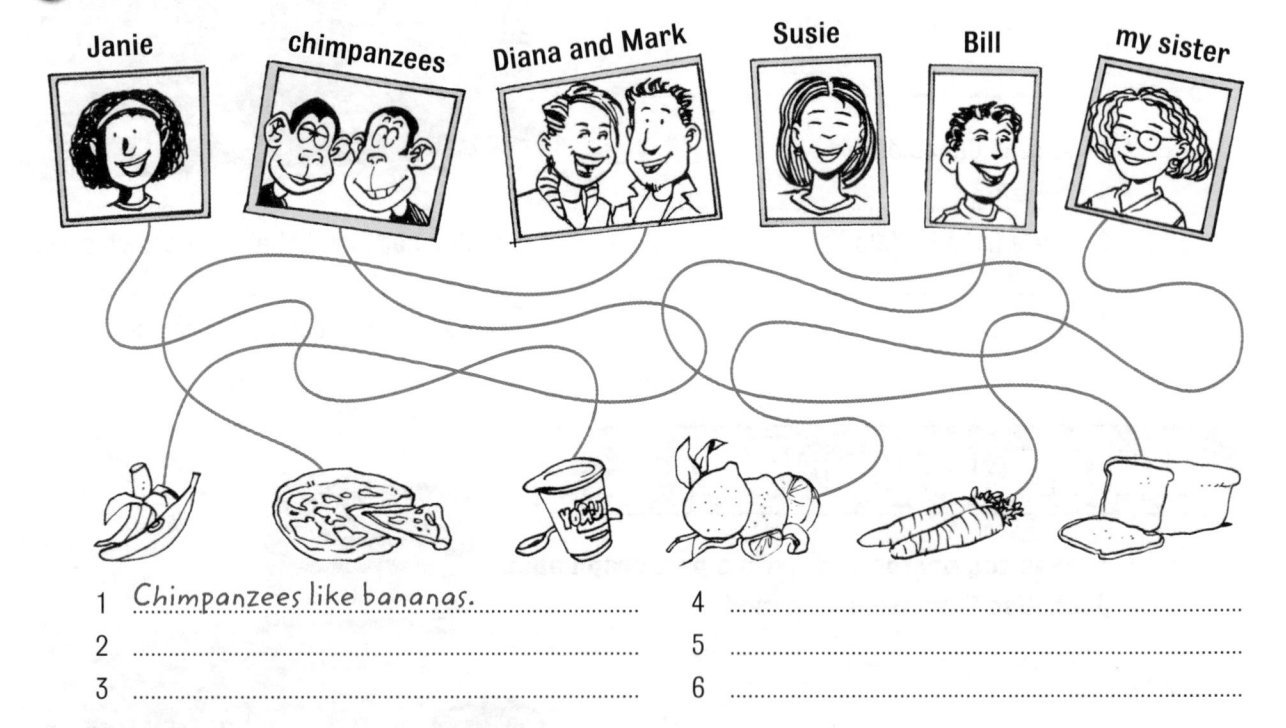

Janie    chimpanzees    Diana and Mark    Susie    Bill    my sister

1. Chimpanzees like bananas.
2. ...........
3. ...........
4. ...........
5. ...........
6. ...........

## 3  Reorder the phrases to make a dialogue.

**Dialogue 1**

- [ ] **Man** OK. Here you go.
- [ ] **Man** Of course. Would you like an egg roll?
- [1] **Girl** Hello. May I have a stir-fry and rice, please?
- [ ] **Girl** Um, yes, thank you.

**Dialogue 2**

- [ ] **Boy** No, thanks. Just plain cheese.
- [ ] **Boy** Thank you.
- [1] **Boy** Hi. May I have a slice of pizza, please?
- [ ] **Woman** Sure. Would you like pepperoni?
- [ ] **Woman** You're welcome.
- [ ] **Woman** Alright. Here you go.

# Language Focus

## Vocabulary Food

**1** Find and circle the names of 12 foods. Then write them under the correct picture.

```
S T R A B E R R I T O S
S T R A W B E R R Y S P
C A I R R O G T I O A I
A C C A B B G I C G N N
B R E A D O S K A U D A
B V E R Y U I H S R W C
A I B T H I L A D T I H
G B A F(C A R R O T)C H
E N N I C F R E A M H G
O H A M B U R G E R S R
S A N D W I O N I O N S
B R A E D A W B I K O N
```

❶ ................
❷ ................
❸ ................
❹ ................
❺ ................
❻ ................
❼ ................
❽ ................
❾ ................
❿ ................
⓫ ................
⓬ ................

## Polite requests

**2** Complete the dialogue using the words below. Then listen and check.

> here   stir-fry   banana   like   thanks   can

**Server**  Hello. What would you ¹................?
**James**  Can I have a ²................, please?
**Server**  Of course. Would you like rice, too?
**James**  Yes, thank you.
**Server**  Would you like a ³................?
**James**  No, ⁴................, but ⁵................ I have a yogurt, please?
**Server**  Sure. ⁶................ you go.
**James**  Thanks.

## Sounds right /ɜ/ and /ɔ/

**3** Listen and write the words in the correct place.

/ɜ/  work  ................  ................  ................  ................
/ɔ/  walk  ................  ................  ................  ................

UNIT 5  109

# Grammar

## Simple present Affirmative

**1** Complete the table with the correct form of *like*.

| I | ¹ like | |
|---|---|---|
| You | ² .......... | |
| He/She/It | ³ .......... | chocolate. |
| We | ⁴ .......... | |
| You | ⁵ .......... | |
| They | ⁶ .......... | |

**2** Circle the correct verb form.

1. I *read* / *reads* magazines on Sunday.
2. Our dog *sleep* / *sleeps* all day!
3. We *live* / *lives* in Mexico City.
4. My father *speak* / *speaks* English.
5. You *know* / *knows* the answer.
6. My brother and sister *love* / *loves* ice cream.
7. My brother *like* / *likes* to watch sports.
8. My mother *teach* / *teaches* in a school.

**3** Complete the sentences using the correct form of the verb in parentheses.

1. John ...*watches*... videos at home. (watch)
2. Our cat .................. in the sun. (relax)
3. My sister is always late, so she .................. to school. (hurry)
4. When we're on vacation, our dog .................. us. (miss)
5. My father .................. the dishes on Sundays. (wash)
6. Mom .................. grocery shopping on Thursdays. (go)

**4** Complete the sentences with the correct form of the verb below.

   go    play    help    wash

1. Our cat ...*plays*... soccer!
2. I .................. games on the computer in the evening. 
3. I .................. my sister with her homework. 
4. And my sister .................. me to clean my bike. 
5. We .................. the car on the weekend. 
6. We .................. to the movies on Fridays. 
7. My father .................. to work at seven o'clock every morning. 
8. And on Sundays, my sister .................. the dog!

## Adverbs of frequency

**5** Put the adverbs of frequency in descending order.

> always   usually   sometimes
> ~~never~~   often

| 100% | .................... |
|------|----------------------|
|      | .................... |
|      | .................... |
|      | .................... |
| 0%   | ......never........ |

**6** Reorder the words and write the sentences.

1 never / she / music / listens / to
  *She never listens to music.*

2 sometimes / rains / it
  ....................................................

3 we / the / usually / door / close
  ....................................................

4 late / my / is / always / brother
  ....................................................

5 to / often / they / place / come / my
  ....................................................

6 on / have / Fridays / we / test / a / always
  ....................................................

7 exercises / easy / usually / the / are
  ....................................................

8 buy / I / never / clothes / expensive
  ....................................................

**7** Rewrite the sentences and put the adverb in the correct place.

1 She answers the phone. (never)
  *She never answers the phone.*

2 My parents are angry with me. (sometimes)
  ....................................................

3 I win the competitions. (usually)
  ....................................................

4 It rains on the weekend. (often)
  ....................................................

5 My mother gets up early. (always)
  ....................................................

6 We watch DVDs on Sunday afternoons. (always)
  ....................................................

7 The ice cream from that store is very good. (usually)
  ....................................................

**8** Look at the table. Complete the sentences with an adverb of frequency and the correct form of the verb.

| ✓✓✓✓ | = always |
|------|----------|
| ✓✓✓✗ | = usually |
| ✓✓✗✗ | = often |
| ✓✗✗✗ | = sometimes |
| ✗✗✗✗ | = never |

1 My cat / ✓✓✓✓ / sleep / on my bed
  *My cat always sleeps on my bed.*

2 She / ✗✗✗✗ / chase / birds
  ....................................................

3 She / be / ✓✓✗✗ / hungry
  ....................................................

4 She / ✓✗✗✗ / watch / TV
  ....................................................

5 She / ✓✓✓✗ / stay out all night
  ....................................................

# Skills

## Listening

**1** Listen and write the number of the dialogue in the correct picture. There are three to choose from.

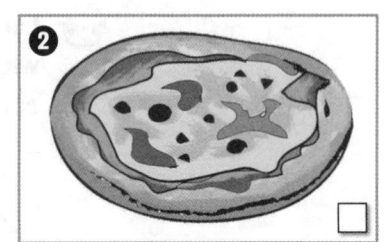

**2** Complete the dialogue with the words below. Then listen and check.

> cheesy   favorite   always   loves   apple   hate   love

**Billy** What day is it today?
**Anna** It's Friday. Why?
**Billy** Friday? Great. I ¹.................. Fridays.
**Anna** Really?
**Billy** Yeah. We ².................. have fish for dinner on Fridays. I think it's my ³.................. food.
**Anna** Fish is your favorite food?
**Billy** Yes. And for dessert we have ⁴.................. pie and ice cream. Mmm!
**Anna** Well, that isn't <u>my</u> favorite food.

**Billy** OK. What <u>is</u> your favorite?
**Anna** Pasta!
**Billy** Pasta? Oh no! I ⁵.................. pasta. It's horrible!
**Anna** No it isn't! I love it and my brother ⁶.................. it too. ⁷.................. pasta is delicious!
**Billy** You're crazy.
**Anna** Bye Billy. Go home and eat your Friday-night fish!
**Billy** OK! See you later, Anna.

## Writing for your Portfolio

**3** Write about your favorite different kinds of foods and how often you eat them.

## Reading

**4** Read the paragraph below about Jenny, Harry, and Sharon's favorite foods.

# Food and the American teenager

We asked three American teenagers about what they usually eat. Here are their answers.

**Harry:** My favorite food has got to be pizza! It's delicious. I sometimes make my own pizza, with super-thin crust and piles of cheese. Yum. I like other things, though, like pasta, and I even like to eat salad from our salad bar at school. It's really good!

**Jenny:** I live in the southwest part of the United States. There is a large Mexican influence here, so we eat a lot of Mexican food. Tacos and burritos are some of my favorites. I always prefer salsa over ketchup! I like a little spice in my food.

I love oranges and strawberries, too. Strawberries and ice cream are great! It's hot here all year, so you can always eat ice cream.

**Sharon:** I think I eat the same things as most other teenagers. I like pizza, pasta, and hamburgers. But I like other things, too. For example, I <u>love</u> fruit for breakfast! I always eat bananas and drink orange juice.

My brother is 16 and he likes Chinese food. He always goes to a Chinese restaurant on the weekend and eats things like stir-fried chicken and rice. His friends love it, too, but <u>my</u> friends and I go to a pizza place on Friday nights. It's really good!

**5** Decide if the sentences are T (True) or F (False).

1. Harry always makes his own pizza.   T / F
2. Sharon's brother hates Chinese food.   T / F
3. The salad bar in Harry's school is awful.   T / F
4. Jenny loves ketchup.   T / F
5. Sharon eats bananas for breakfast.   T / F
6. Harry likes pasta.   T / F
7. Jenny likes strawberries and ice cream.   T / F

**1** Match the questions to the answers.

1 What time is it?
2 What's the matter?
3 Does it start at seven?
4 Do you want a sandwich?
5 When does the show start?
6 Do you like football?

a No, thanks.
b It starts at seven o'clock.
c It's ten past six.
d No, I don't!
e I'm bored.
f Yes, it does.

**2** Reorder the phrases to make a dialogue. Then listen and check.

☐ **Sally** Why? What's the matter?
☐ **Sally** Oh. Do you want a sandwich?
☐ **Sally** OK. Bye Mike!
[1] **Sally** Hi, Mike. How are you?
☐ **Mike** Oh no! I'm late! The football game starts at a quarter past five!
☐ **Sally** It's ten past five. Why?
☐ **Mike** Yes, please. What time is it?
☐ **Mike** Not very good.
☐ **Mike** I'm hungry!

**3** Match each picture to the correct time.

☐ It's seven o'clock.
☐ It's ten o'clock.
[1] It's two thirty.
☐ It's ten past nine.
☐ It's twenty past eleven.
☐ It's a quarter to three.
☐ It's six thirty.
☐ It's twenty to eleven.
☐ It's ten to nine.
☐ It's a quarter past three.

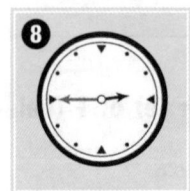

## Sounds right  Mute letters

**4** Listen and circle the mute letter.

1 sandwich    2 walk    3 listen    4 answer    5 friend    6 half

# Language Focus

## Vocabulary Daily activities

**1** Complete the puzzle with the correct verbs.

1 ............................. to music
2 ............................. the piano / video games
3 ............................. friends / family
4 ............................. the Net
5 ............................. the dog for a walk
6 ............................. the cat / the dog
7 ............................. out with friends

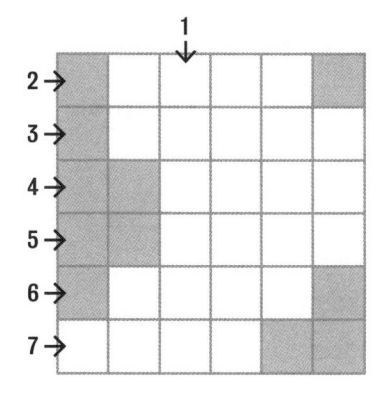

## Talking about routines

**2** Complete the sentences about Jack.

1. Saturday morning
2. Monday evening
3. Sunday afternoon
4. Saturday evening
5. Friday evening
6. Sunday morning
7. Saturday afternoon
8. Sunday evening

1 On Saturday morning he plays the piano.
2 ...................................................................................
3 ...................................................................................
4 ...................................................................................
5 ...................................................................................
6 ...................................................................................
7 ...................................................................................
8 ...................................................................................

UNIT 6  115

# Grammar

## Simple present Negative

**1** Write *don't* or *doesn't*.

| Affirmative | Negative |
|---|---|
| I know. | I ¹............... know. |
| You know. | You ²............... know. |
| He knows. | He ³............... know. |
| She knows. | She ⁴............... know. |
| It knows. | It ⁵ *doesn't* know. |

| Affirmative | Negative |
|---|---|
| We know. | We ⁶............... know. |
| You know. | You ⁷............... know. |
| They know. | They ⁸............... know. |

**2** Complete the sentences with *don't* or *doesn't*.

1 He *doesn't* like spinach.
2 They ............... live in a big house. 
3 I ............... know the answer. 
4 She ............... go to our school. 
5 We ............... understand! 
6 It ............... eat meat. 
7 He ............... speak English. 
8 You ............... play very well. 

**3** Complete the sentences with the negative form of the verb.

1 He likes apples, but he *doesn't* *like* strawberries.
2 She speaks Spanish, but she ............... ............... French.
3 I understand algebra, but I ............... ............... geometry.
4 They eat chicken, but they ............... ............... pork.
5 It rains in the winter here, but it ............... ............... in the summer.
6 You watch DVDs, but you ............... ............... television.

**4** Write true sentences about yourself.

1 I / not like *fish*   I don't like fish.
2 My friend / not speak ...............
3 I / not play ...............
4 My mother and father / not like ...............

## Simple present Questions and short answers

**5** Complete the table with *do*, *don't*, *does*, or *doesn't*.

| Question | Affirmative short answer | Negative short answer |
|---|---|---|
| Do I read a lot? | Yes, you do. | No, you don't. |
| 1 .......... you speak French? | Yes, I do. | No, I 11 .......... |
| 2 .......... he live here? | Yes, he 6 .......... | No, he doesn't. |
| Does she like you? | Yes, she 7 .......... | No, she 12 .......... |
| 3 .......... it open at noon? | Yes, it does. | No, it 13 .......... |
| 4 .......... we understand? | Yes, we 8 .......... | No, we don't. |
| Do you play volleyball? | Yes, you 9 .......... | No, you 14 .......... |
| 5 .......... they know us? | Yes, they 10 .......... | No, they 15 .......... |

**6** Write questions and answers.

**1** ¡Hola!
Michael / speak Spanish?
*Does Michael speak Spanish?*
Yes, he does.

**2** Sara / eat meat?
..........................?
..........................

**3** they / know the way?
..........................?
..........................

**4** your dog / chase cats?
..........................?
..........................

**7** Answer the questions.

1 Do you like football?
   *Yes I do. / No, I don't.*

2 Do your parents like sports?
   ..........................

3 Does your best friend speak English?
   ..........................

## Object pronouns

**8** Complete the table with the correct object pronoun below.

us   them   her   you   ~~it~~   him   me

| Subject | Object |
|---|---|
| I | 1 .......... |
| you | 2 .......... |
| he | 3 .......... |
| she | 4 .......... |
| it | 5 *it* |
| we | 6 .......... |
| they | 7 .......... |

**9** Write the correct object pronoun.

1 I love the *30 Rock* TV show. Do you like ....*it*....?
2 She's my new friend. Come and meet ..........!
3 Go away. I don't want to talk to ..........!
4 I like James, but he doesn't like ..........
5 He's really nice. Do you like .......... , too?
6 Tell .......... —we really want to know!

# Skills

## Reading

**1** **Read the letter and answer the questions.**

1 Where does Harry the hamster live?
...............................................................

2 What does Mandy give Harry, his brother, and his sister?
...............................................................

3 How does Mandy carry the hamsters to school?
...............................................................

4 What does Bob feed Harry?
...............................................................

---

Dear Aunt Olivia,

I've got a problem. I'm a hamster. I live in a small cage with my brother and my sister. Our owners are a boy and a girl. The girl's name is Mandy. We like Mandy a lot. She gives us a lot of nice food. She sometimes feeds us chocolate! She often plays with us. She sometimes carries us to school in her backpack. Yes, we love her. Mandy's great.

The problem is Bob, the boy. We don't like Bob very much. He doesn't give us nice food. He only feeds us spiders. We don't eat spiders, of course.

What can I do?

Harry the hamster

---

**2** **Read Olivia's answer and complete it using the words below.**

> eat    doesn't know    doesn't understand    don't eat    loves

Dear Harry,

Thank you for your letter. It's great that you like Mandy a lot. It's great that she
¹........................... you and you love Mandy.

Bob isn't bad. He likes you, but he ²........................... hamsters. He thinks you
³........................... spiders! He ⁴........................... that hamsters ⁵........................... spiders.

Love,
Aunt Olivia

## Listening

**3** **Listen and answer the questions about this boy's pet.**

1 What is it? ...............................................
2 What's his name? ...............................................
3 How often does the boy feed him? ...............
4 What does he eat? ...............................................

5 What doesn't he eat? ...............................................
6 Does the boy take him for walks? ...............
7 Where does he live? ...............................................

**4** Read and complete the dialogue with the words below. Then listen and check.

> do   o'clock   likes   like   usually   joke   afternoon   take

**Sarah** Do you ¹.................. roller-skating, Mike?
**Mike** Yes, I do. I go roller-skating every Friday!
**Sarah** Oh really? Where?
**Mike** Well, I go to the park with my friends after school, around four ².................. . We roller-skate for about an hour, and then we go home.
**Sarah** I go roller-skating, too, but I go on Saturday. I go shopping in the morning, and then I ³.................. our dog for a walk. In the ⁴.................., I go to the park with my mother.
**Mike** Your mother?!
**Sarah** Yes, she ⁵.................. roller-skating, too, and she's really good!
**Mike** What do you do on Saturday evening?
**Sarah** Oh, I ⁶.................. go out with my friends. We go to the movies or a restaurant. And you?
**Mike** On Saturday I ⁷.................. my homework.
**Sarah** What? Is that a ⁸.................. ?
**Mike** No! It's true!
**Sarah** Oh, Mike! Get a life!

## Reading

**5** Read the description about Francesca's weekend and answer the questions.

> On Friday afternoon, after school, I usually surf the Net or listen to music. In the evening I often go to the movies with my friends.
>
> On Saturday morning, I get up (late!) and have breakfast. Then I take the dog for a walk. In the afternoon, I watch TV (usually a football game). In the evening I go to my best friend's place. We sometimes play video games or we talk.
>
> On Sunday morning I do my homework. Then I listen to music or watch TV. On Sunday evening I surf the Net again or read a book.

1 Where does she often go on Friday evening?
   _To the movies._
2 When does she take the dog for a walk?
   ...................................................................
3 What does she watch on Saturday?
   ...................................................................
4 What does she do on Sunday morning?
   ...................................................................
5 When does she surf the Net?
   ...................................................................

## Writing for your Portfolio

**6** Write a paragraph about your weekend. Use the description from Exercise 5 to help you.

# Wordlist

## Starter section

apple /ˈæpəl/
chicken /ˈtʃɪkən/
eight /eɪt/
eighteen /eɪˈtin/
eleven /ɪˈlɛvən/
favorite /ˈfeɪv(ə)rət/
fifteen /fɪfˈtin/
five /faɪv/
food /fud/
four /fɔr/
fourteen /fɔrtin/
friend /frɛnd/
friendly /ˈfrɛndli/
from /frʌm/
fruit /frut/
good afternoon /gʊd æftərnun/
good evening /gʊd ˈivnɪŋ/
good morning /gʊd ˈmɔrnɪŋ/
good night /gʊd ˈnaɪt/
goodbye /gʊd ˈbaɪ/
great /greɪt/
hamburger /ˈhæmbərgər/
hamster /ˈhæmstər/
hello /hɛˈloʊ/
her /hɛːr/
hi /haɪ/
his /hɪz/
horse /hɔrs/
house /haʊs/
late /leɪt/
nice /naɪs/
nine /naɪn/
nineteen /naɪnˈtin/
number /ˈnʌmbər/
one /wʌn/
pet /pet/
right /raɪt/
scared /skɛrd/
seven /ˈsɛvən/
seventeen /sɛvənˈtin/
six /sɪks/
sixteen /sɪkˈstin/
ten /tɛn/
thanks /θæŋks/
thirteen /θɜrˈtin/
three /θri/
twenty /ˈtwɛnti/
twenty-one /twɛnti ˈwʌn/
two /tu/
where /wɛr/
wrong /rɔŋ/

## Unit 1

activity /ækˈtɪvəti/
angry /ˈæŋgri/
another /əˈnʌðər/
bad /bæd/
band /bænd/
beautiful /ˈbyutɪfəl/
bored /bɔrd/
boy /bɔɪ/
bus stop /ˈbʌs stɑp/
busy /ˈbɪzi/
bye /baɪ/
car /kɑr/
city /ˈsɪti/
cold /koʊld/
day /deɪ/
download /ˈdaʊnloʊd/
duck /dʌk/
during /ˈdʊrɪŋ/
excited /ɪkˈsaɪtəd/
fantastic /fænˈtæstɪk/
fast /fæst/
feel /fil/
fun /fʌn/
happy /ˈhæpi/
here /hɪr/
homework /ˈhoʊmwərk/
hot /hɑt/
hungry /ˈhʌŋgri/
in front of /ɪn ˈfrʌnt əv/
meet /mit/
museum /myuˈziəm/
nervous /ˈnərvəs/
new /nyu/
one /wʌn/
sad /sæd/
school /skul/
select /sɪˈlɛkt/
shopping /ˈʃɑpɪŋ/
sorry /ˈsɑri/
tired /ˈtaɪərd/
tomorrow /təˈmɑroʊ/
town /taʊn/
type /taɪp/
week /wik/
weekend /wikˈɛnd/

## Unit 2

actor /ˈæktə(r)/
behind /bɪˈhaɪnd/
board /bɔrd/
capital /ˈkæpɪtəl/
CD player /ˌsi di ˌpleɪər/
chair /tʃɛr/
to come /kʌm/
door /dɔr/
empty /ˈɛmpti/
floor /flɔr/
in /ɪn/
lake /leɪk/
to laugh /læf/
to look /lʊk/
mountain /ˈmaʊntən/
next to /ˈnɛkst tə/
on /ɑn/
open /ˈoʊpən/
pencil case /ˈpɛnsl keɪs/
person / people /pɛrsən/ /pipəl/
phone number /foʊn nʌmbər/
quiet /kwaɪət/
right /raɪt/
river /ˈrɪvər/
to sit /sɪt/
south /saʊθ/
stadium /ˈsteɪdiəm/
to stand /stænd/
student /ˈstyudənt/
today /təˈdeɪ/
under /ˈʌndər/
watch /wɑtʃ/
why /waɪ/
window /ˈwɪndoʊ/

## Unit 3

armchair /ˈɑrmtʃɛr/
bathtub /bɑθ/
bathroom /ˈbæθrum/
bed /bɛd/
bedroom /ˈbɛdrum/
big /bɪg/
bookshelf /ˈbʊkʃɛlf/
campsite /ˈkæmpsaɪt/
children /ˈtʃɪldrən/
closet /ˈklɑzət/
curtains /ˈkɜrtənz/
DVD player /di vi ˈdi ˌpleɪər/
early /ˈɛrli/
eye /aɪ/
famous /ˈfeɪməs/
forest /ˈfɔrəst/
free /fri/
fridge /frɪdʒ/
garage /gəˈrɑdʒ/
hall /hɔl/
hill /hɪl/
hippo /ˈhɪpoʊ/
ideal /aɪˈdi(ə)l/
kitchen /ˈkɪtʃən/
light /laɪt/
living room /ˈlɪvɪŋ rum/
monster /ˈmɑnstər/
owl /aʊl/
place /pleɪs/
pool /pul/
poster /ˈpoʊstər/
ride /raɪd/
sandwich /ˈsæn(d)wɪtʃ/
screen /skrin/
small /smɔl/
sofa /ˈsoʊfə/
square /skwɛr/
stereo /ˈstɛrioʊ/
sure /ʃʊr/
swimming pool /ˈswɪmɪŋ pul/
table /ˈteɪbəl/
tell /tɛl/
theater /ˈθɪətər/
toilet /ˈtɔɪlət/
tree /tri/
trip /trɪp/
unfriendly /ʌnˈfrɛndli/
valley /ˈvæli/
watch /wɑtʃ/
zoo /zu/

## Unit 4

accent /ˈæksənt/
American /əˈmɛrɪkən/
arm /ɑrm/
art /ɑrt/
banana /bəˈnænə/
bear /bɛr/
bicycle /ˈbaɪsɪkəl/
biology /baɪˈɑlədʒi/
Brazil /brəˈzɪl/
Brazilian /brəˈzɪlyən/
chemistry /ˈkɛmɪstri/
China /ˈtʃaɪnə/
Chinese /tʃaɪˈniz/
cool /kul/
crocodile /ˈkrɑkəˌdaɪ(ə)l/
ear /ɪr/
feet /fit/
fingers /ˈfɪŋgərz/
flag /flæg/
food /fud/
foot /fʊt/
frog /frɔg/
geography /dʒiˈɑgrəfi/
gorilla /gəˈrɪlə/
hair /hɛr/
hand /hænd/
head /hɛd/
history /ˈhɪst(ə)ri/
honey /ˈhʌni/
ice cream /ˌaɪs ˈkrim/
Japan /dʒəˈpæn/
Japanese /ˌdʒæpəˈniz/
left /lɛft/
leg /lɛg/
long /lɑŋ/
look /lʊk/
mouth /maʊθ/
music /ˈmyuzɪk/
news /nuz/
nose /noʊz/
pen pal /ˈpɛn pæl/
short /ʃɔrt/
shoulder /ˈʃoʊldər/
skateboard /ˈskeɪtbɔrd/
Spanish /ˈspænɪʃ/
tall /tɔl/
teeth /tiθ/
toes /toʊz/
umbrella /əmˈbrɛlə/
the U.S. /ðə ˌyu ɛs/
wide-mouthed /ˈwaɪd maʊðd/

## Unit 5

almost /ˈɔlmoʊst/
always /ˈɔlweɪz/
beef /bif/
bread /brɛd/
bus /bʌs/
buy /baɪ/
cabbage /ˈkæbɪdʒ/
candy /ˈkændi/
carrot /ˈkɛrət/
carry /ˈkæri/
cheese /tʃiz/
cherries /ˈtʃɛriz/
chicken /ˈtʃɪkən/
coffee /ˈkɔfi/
corner /ˈkɔrnər/
dear /dɪr/
dinner /ˈdɪnər/
to do /du/
drink /drɪŋk/
egg /ɛgz/
every /ˈɛvri/
father /ˈfɑðər/
fish /fɪʃ/
fishing /ˈfɪʃɪŋ/
fruit /frut/
grapes /greɪps/
hamburger /ˈhæmˌbərgər/
to hate /heɪt/
hot dog /ˈhɑt dɑg/
junk food /ˈdʒʌŋk fud/
to kiss /kɪs/
kiwi /ˈkiwi/
lunch /lʌntʃ/
meat /mit/
milk /mɪlk/
to miss /mɪs/
month /mʌn(t)θ/
never /ˈnɛvər/
noodles /ˈnudəlz/
of course /əv ˈkɔrs/
often /ˈɔfən, ˈɔftən/
once /wʌn(t)s/
onion /ˈʌnyən/
orange /ˈɑrɪndʒ/
orange juice /ˈɑrɪndʒ ˌdʒus/
pork /pɔrk/
potato /pəˈteɪtoʊ/
to relax /rɪˈlæks/
restaurant /ˈrɛst(ə)rɑnt/
rice /raɪs/
sausage /ˈsɔsɪdʒ/
sometimes /ˈsʌmtaɪmz/
soup /sup/
spinach /ˈspɪnɪtʃ/
steak /steɪk/
strawberry /ˈstrɔbɛri/
to take /teɪk/
tomato /təˈmeɪtoʊ/
true /tru/
usually /ˈyuʒəwəli/
vegetable /ˈvɛdʒtəbəl/
to wash /wɔʃ/
work /wɛrk/

## Unit 6

answer /ˈæn(t)sər/
away /əˈweɪ/
baby /ˈbeɪbi/
before /bɪˈfɔr/
to begin /bɪˈgɪn/
boring /ˈbɔrɪŋ/
brother /ˈbrʌðər/
to clean /klin/
clock /klɑk/
to cut /kʌt/
end /ɛnd/
family /ˈfæmli/
farm /fɑrm/
to feed /fid/
friend /frɛnd/
to get up /gɛt ˈʌp/
to go /goʊ/
grass /græs/
gym /dʒɪm/
to hang out /hæŋ ˈaʊt/
to have breakfast /hæv ˈbrɛkfəst/
to hope /hoʊp/
hour /ˈaʊ(ə)r/
interesting /ˈɪnt(ə)rəstɪŋ/
joke /dʒoʊk/
to know /noʊ/
to leave /liv/
life /laɪf/
to listen to /ˈlɪsən tə/
to live /lɪv/
o'clock /əˈklɑk/
parents /ˈpɛrənts/
piano /piˈænoʊ/
to play /pleɪ/
problem /ˈprɑbləm/
to read /rid/
rhyme /raɪm/
to ride a horse /ˌraɪd ə ˈhɔrs/
rock /rɑk/
roller-skating /ˈroʊlər ˌskeɪtɪŋ/
romantic /roʊˈmæntɪk/
same /seɪm/
to speak /spik/
to start /stɑrt/
to surf /sərf/
to talk /tɔk/
thing /θɪŋ/
to understand /ˌʌndərˈstænd/
village /ˈvɪlɪdʒ/
to walk /wɔrk/
to want /wɑnt/
water buffalo /ˈwɔtər ˌbʌfəloʊ/

## Pronunciation guide

### Vowels

| | |
|---|---|
| /i/ | r**ea**l, scr**ee**n |
| /ɪ/ | d**i**sh, s**i**t |
| /ɛ/ | ch**e**ss, b**e**d |
| /æ/ | b**a**d, t**a**xi |
| /ʌ/ | m**u**st, d**o**ne |
| /ʊ/ | g**oo**d, f**u**ll |
| /u/ | ch**oo**se, vi**ew** |
| /ə/ | dr**a**matic, th**e** |
| /ɑ/ | st**o**p, **o**pera |
| /ɔ/ | s**aw**, d**au**ghter |

### Vowels + /r/

| | |
|---|---|
| /ər/ | f**ir**st, sh**ir**t |
| /ɑr/ | c**ar** |
| /ɔr/ | h**or**se |
| /ɛr/ | th**eir** |
| /ʊr/ | t**our**ist |
| /ɪr/ | **ear** |

### Diphthongs

| | |
|---|---|
| /eɪ/ | pl**ay**, tr**ai**n |
| /aɪ/ | **i**ce, n**igh**t |
| /ɔɪ/ | empl**oy**er, n**oi**sy |
| /aʊ/ | h**ou**se, d**ow**nload |
| /oʊ/ | n**o**, wind**ow** |

### Consonants

| | |
|---|---|
| /p/ | **p**ush |
| /b/ | **b**ank |
| /t/ | **t**ime |
| /d/ | **d**iary |
| /k/ | **c**arpet |
| /g/ | bi**g** |
| /f/ | sur**f** |
| /v/ | **v**ery |
| /θ/ | **th**in |
| /ð/ | **th**at |
| /s/ | **s**it |
| /z/ | **z**ero |
| /ʃ/ | **sh**ine |
| /ʒ/ | mea**s**ure |
| /h/ | **h**ot |
| /w/ | **w**ater |
| /tʃ/ | **ch**air |
| /dʒ/ | **j**oke |
| /m/ | **m**ore |
| /n/ | s**n**ow |
| /ŋ/ | si**ng** |
| /r/ | **r**ing |
| /l/ | sma**ll** |
| /y/ | **y**ou |

# Grammar Review

## Subject pronouns
Starter Section

| Singular | Plural |
|---|---|
| I | we |
| you | you |
| he / she / it | they |

We always write **I** with a capital letter. *I am Filipino.*

**You** is for the second person singular and second person plural. *You are a student. You are students.*

**He** is for a male. *He is a teacher.*

**She** is for a female. *She is a doctor.*

**It** is neutral and refers to animals or things. *That's the house. It is big.*

**They** is for male and female. *They are girls. They are boys.*

## Simple present of *be*
Starter Section, Unit 1

| Affirmative | Short form | Negative | Short form | Questions | Short answers |
|---|---|---|---|---|---|
| I am | I'm | I am not | I'm not | Am I? | Yes, I am. / No, I'm not. |
| you are | you're | you are not | you aren't | Are you? | Yes, you are. / No, you aren't. |
| he is | he's | he is not | he isn't | Is he? | Yes, he is. / No, he isn't. |
| she is | she's | she is not | she isn't | Is she? | Yes, she is. / No, she isn't. |
| it is | it's | it is not | it isn't | Is it? | Yes, it is. / No, it isn't. |
| we are | we're | we are not | we aren't | Are we? | Yes, we are. / No, we aren't. |
| you are | you're | you are not | you aren't | Are you? | Yes, you are. / No, you aren't. |
| they are | they're | they are not | they aren't | Are they? | Yes, they are. / No, they aren't. |

In English, the subject of a verb must always be expressed:
*She's my sister.* (**Not:** *Is my sister.*)

Short forms are used in spoken English and in informal written English.

## Plural and irregular nouns
Starter Section

Add **s** to regular singular nouns to make them plural:
table → table**s**   bed → bed**s**   pen → pen**s**

Add **es** to nouns ending in **s**, **sh**, **ss**, **ch**, **o**, **x**, **z**: bus → bus**es**   wish → wish**es**
peach → peach**es**   potato → potato**es**   boss → boss**es**   fox → fox**es**

Not all nouns ending in **o** form the plural by adding **es**: piano → piano**s**   photo → photo**s**

For nouns ending in **y** after a consonant, form the plural by changing the **y** into **ies**.
baby → bab**ies**   party → part**ies**

If the **y** follows a vowel, the plural is formed by adding **s** only: boy → boy**s**
Some nouns ending in **f** or **fe** drop the **f** or **fe** and add **ves**: life → li**ves**   wife → wi**ves**

### Irregular plurals

child → child**ren**   man → m**e**n   woman → wom**e**n
foot → f**ee**t   tooth → t**ee**th   mouse → m**i**ce

## Possessive adjectives

Starter Section, Unit 1

| Singular | Plural |
|---|---|
| my | our |
| your | your |
| his<br>her<br>its | their |

**his** refers to a male possessor. *Tom's dog. His dog.*
**her** refers to a female possessor. *Sue's dog. Her dog.*
**its** refers to a neutral possessor. *The house's door. Its door.*

## Question words  Who/Where/Why/What/What color?

Units 1 and 2

**Who?** (for people)   **What?** (for things)   **Where?** (for places)   **What color?** (for color)

**Why?** is used to ask a question and is usually answered by **because**:
*Why is your friend here?*   **Because** *he wants to speak to me.*

## Prepositions

Unit 2

| Prepositions of place | Prepositions of movement |
|---|---|
| at | to |
| in / inside | into |
| on | through / across |
| over | from |
| under | out of |
| out / outside | |

## Imperatives

Unit 2

The imperative is used to give orders and instructions, or to make suggestions.
It has the same form as the infinitive without "to":
*To come → Come here!*   *To go → Go away!*

The negative is formed by putting **don't** before the imperative:
*Don't be silly!*   *Don't go away!*

## Adjectives

Unit 3

Adjectives never change in English. They usually come before their nouns:
*Mary is a **nice** girl.*   *They are **nice** girls.*

Numbers come before adjectives:
*Here are **three nice** girls.*

## Possessive 's

Unit 3

To indicate possession, we add **'s** to the name of the possessor:
*John**'s** house. That boy**'s** dog.*

If the possessor is a plural noun ending in **s**, an apostrophe (**'**) is added:
*The students' books.*

124   GRAMMAR REVIEW

## *there is / there are*  Unit 3

|  | Affirmative | Negative | Questions | Short answers |
|---|---|---|---|---|
| **Singular** | there is (there's) | there is not (there isn't) | is there …? | Yes, there is. / No, there isn't. |
| **Plural** | there are | there are not (there aren't) | are there …? | Yes, there are. / No, there aren't. |

We use **there is** / **there are** to say that something exists. In spoken English **there is** can be shortened to **there's**.
**There is** *(There's) a lamp on the table.*   **There are** *some books on the table.*

## Articles  *A / an / the*  Units 4 and 10

**Use:**
**A** before a consonant or a voiced **h**: *a **t**eacher   a **p**encil case   a **h**ouse*
**An** before a vowel: *an **a**pple   an **e**lephant   an **i**ce cream   an **o**range   an **u**mbrella*
or a silent **h**: *an **h**our*

## Simple present of *have*  Unit 4

| Affirmative | Negative | Short form |
|---|---|---|
| I have | I do not have | I don't have |
| you have | you do not have | you don't have |
| he has | he does not have | he doesn't have |
| she has | she does not have | she doesn't have |
| it has | it does not have | it doesn't have |
| we have | we do not have | we don't have |
| you have | you do not have | you don't have |
| they have | they do not have | they don't have |

| Questions | Short answers |
|---|---|
| Do I have? | Yes, I do. / No, I don't. |
| Do you have? | Yes, you do. / No, you don't. |
| Does he have? | Yes, he does. / No, he doesn't. |
| Does she have? | Yes, she does. / No, she doesn't. |
| Does it have? | Yes, it does. / No, it doesn't. |
| Do we have? | Yes, we do. / No, we don't. |
| Do you have? | Yes, you do. / No, you don't. |
| Do they have? | Yes, they do. / No, they don't. |

## Adverbs of frequency
Unit 5

Adverbs of frequency always come before the *simple present*:
*He **always** stays at home.*   *He **never** goes on vacation.*

but follow *to be* and modal verbs:
*He is **always** nice.*   *He can **sometimes** be angry.*

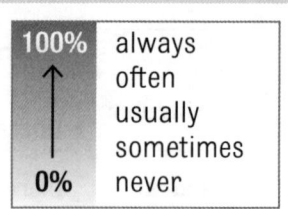

| 100% | always |
| --- | --- |
| ↑ | often |
| | usually |
| | sometimes |
| 0% | never |

## Simple present
Units 5 and 6

| Affirmative | Negative | Questions | Short answers |
| --- | --- | --- | --- |
| I work | I don't work | Do I work? | Yes, I do. / No, I don't. |
| you work | you don't work | Do you work? | Yes, you do. / No, you don't. |
| he works | he doesn't work | Does he work? | Yes, he does. / No, he doesn't. |
| she works | she doesn't work | Does she work? | Yes, she does. / No, she doesn't. |
| it works | it doesn't work | Does it work? | Yes, it does. / No, it doesn't. |
| we work | we don't work | Do we work? | Yes, we do. / No, we don't. |
| you work | you don't work | Do you work? | Yes, you do. / No, you don't. |
| they work | they don't work | Do they work? | Yes, they do. / No, they don't. |

We use the *simple present* for habits and routines. We also use the simple present with adverbs of frequency such as **often** and **usually**, and with time expressions such as **in the morning** and **every day**.

In the *simple present* add an **s** for the third person singular:  work → work**s**

As for nouns, verbs ending in **s**, **ss**, **ch**, **x**, and **o** form the third person singular by adding **es**:
*he wish**es**   she go**es**   he pass**es**   she fax**es***

Verbs ending in **y** after a consonant form the third person by changing the **y** into **ies**:  *she stud**ies***

If the **y** follows a vowel, the third person is formed regularly by adding **s** only:  *he play**s***

The negative of the *simple present* is formed with **do not** (short form **don't**), or in the third person **does not** (short form **doesn't**) + infinitive without "to."
*I **don't** go to school.*   *He **doesn't** study hard.*

The interrogative is formed with **do / does** + infinitive without "to."
***Do** you study hard?*   ***Does** he go to school?*

## Object pronouns
Unit 6

| Singular | Plural |
| --- | --- |
| me | us |
| you | you |
| him / her / it | them |

*Object pronouns* are used as direct objects after verbs and as complements after prepositions.
*I like **her**.*   *I see **them** every week.*
*Look at **him**.*   *They are with **us**.*

## Instruções de uso do CD-ROM

### Instalação

Insira o CD-ROM **American MORE!** no compartimento de CD e siga na tela as instruções de instalação.

Se as instruções não aparecerem na tela, entre em *Meu Computador*, clique em D (ou no *drive* apropriado). Em seguida dê um duplo-clique no ícone *American More!* para iniciar a instalação.

Para usar o CD-ROM, dê um duplo-clique no atalho **American MORE!** criado na área de trabalho.

### Conteúdo do CD-ROM

Exercícios interativos complementares para prática de vocabulário, gramática, pronúncia, leitura, compreensão oral e produção escrita, além de jogos divertidos. Clique em uma das unidades (Starter-12) e selecione uma das atividades para começar.

### Configurações de sistema recomendadas

| |
|---|
| Windows 2000/XP/: 256MB RAM (mín. 512 MB) |
| Windows Vista/7: 1GB RAM (mín. 2GB) |

### Suporte

Para resolver problemas técnicos relacionados ao uso deste CD-ROM, acesse: www.cambridge.org/elt/multimedia/help

Termos e condições de uso para o **American MORE!** CD-ROM

**1 Licença**

(a) A Cambridge University Press e a Editora Ática concedem licença de uso desse CD-ROM (i) em um único computador para uma ou mais pessoas em momentos diferentes, ou (ii) para uma única pessoa em um ou mais computadores (contanto que o CD-ROM seja usado somente em um computador por vez e por apenas um usuário).

(b) Em relação ao conteúdo desse CD-ROM, o usuário não poderá: (i) copiar ou autorizar a cópia, (ii) traduzir, (iii) inverter a ordem ou alterar a estrutura, (iv) transferir, vender, delegar ou ceder qualquer parte, ou (v) disponibilizar em uma rede ou servidor.

**2 Direitos Autorais**

Todo conteúdo do CD-ROM é protegido pela lei de direito autoral e propriedade intelectual. O usuário adquire apenas o direito de uso do CD-ROM sem qualquer outro direito sobre seu conteúdo, expresso ou oculto, que não aqueles expressos na licença.

**3 Obrigações**

No âmbito jurídico, a Cambridge University Press e a Editora Ática não se responsabilizam por danos ou perdas de qualquer natureza decorrentes do uso desse produto ou de quaisquer erros e problemas no CD-ROM. Em todos os casos as obrigações das editoras se limitam ao valor real pago pelo produto.

| Workbook 1 – Audio CD ||||||||
|---|---|---|---|---|---|---|---|
| **Track** | **Time** | **Track** | **Time** | **Track** | **Time** | **Track** | **Time** |
| 1. | 0'52" | 13. | 0'35" | 25. | 0'56" | 37. | 1'12" |
| 2. | 0'45" | 14. | 1'13" | 26. | 1'15" | 38. | 1'33" |
| 3. | 1'09" | 15. | 1'10" | 27. | 0'52" | 39. | 0'38" |
| 4. | 1'09" | 16. | 1'08" | 28. | 2'19" | 40. | 1'31" |
| 5. | 0'33" | 17. | 0'44" | 29. | 1'37" | 41. | 0'58" |
| 6. | 0'58" | 18. | 1'06" | 30. | 0'40" | 42. | 0'41" |
| 7. | 0'40" | 19. | 0'44" | 31. | 1'23" | 43. | 0'40" |
| 8. | 0'42" | 20. | 1'11" | 32. | 0'55" | 44. | 1'37" |
| 9. | 0'51" | 21. | 1'11" | 33. | 1'09" | 45. | 0'29" |
| 10. | 0'36" | 22. | 1'23" | 34. | 1'02" | 46. | 0'39" |
| 11. | 1'16" | 23. | 1'46" | 35. | 2'11" | 47. | 1'14" |
| 12. | 0'46" | 24. | 0'45" | 36. | 0'39" | | |
| **Total Duration: 49min23s** ||||||||